I0080128

The Real Confident You:

Advice From a 20 Something Suicide Survivor

By Pat Broe

Copyright © 2024 by Pat Broe

All rights reserved. No part of this book may be reproduced in any form on by an electronic or mechanical means, including information storage and retrieval systems, without permission in writing from the publisher, except by a reviewer who may quote brief passages in a review.

This Book is Dedicated to all that made it possible:

Kim Broe

Al Broe

Steve Traun

Sara Newman

Ryan Todd

Kristina Ahlers

Sarah Crowley

Blake Bigalk

Tyler Jeffries

Victoria Gail Hopkins

Matt Dorn

Benjamin Krych

Zane Jarecke

Elizabeth Barnet

Michael Lugar

McKaylee Ferguson

Maddie Kiner

Suzanne Zimmer

Alexander Rogers

Nicholas Hayes

Joshua Fields

Luke Radtke

Beth and Pete Goethel

Kelly Goethel

Eric Hanson

Jared Teed

Ross Withington

Betsy Watkins

Corrie King

Joseph Mayer

Kathy Levonaitis

Lorica Jackson

Austin "Buck" Wallert

Searra Anderson

Haley Melby

Bella Linden

Justine Coleman

Alex Murphy

Courtney Brisson

Emma Olson

Kathleen Coughlin

Bailey Babcock

Mariah Deyo

Savannah Sarbacker

Taylor Eddy

Maddi Mcleland

Frankie Rath

Sara Kuhn

Cassie Berenz

Dalton Goethel

Kelli Kampert

Hudson Greenwood

Leighton Wegener

Emily Desanto

Anthony Dockendorf

Rachel Anderson

Corissa Miller

Jorgen Erickson

Joe DuBois

Rylee Meyer

Lukas Reuteman

Eli Casey

Zachary Broe

John Zimmer

Jaclyn Levonaitis

Austin Jeffries

Bailee Brandt

Jack Terway

Abby Fishbach

Doug Westerman

Steve Turkington

Peter Ardnt

Greg Manson

Steve Considine

Randy Ebright

Nick Karls

Ryan White

Mitchell Cochran

Rose Miller

Alyssa Fuller

Noah Nelson

Jennifer L Levonaitis

David Packer

Hannah Shuster

Corrie King

Darius Manuel

The Grizzlies

Ryan Ford

Jim, Kari, Graham &

Annie Langkamp

Jarod Schyvinch

Table of Contents

My Story

"No one you can save that can't be saved. Nothing you can do but you can learn how to be you in time. It's easy. All you need is love."
~ The Beatles, All You Need is Love

In 2020 I wrote an article about my suicide attempt. This is that story:

Suicide to Success by Pat Broe

Published: 21 February, 2020

A couple months ago, I accepted my dream job and am in the process of planning my move to a beachfront condo in Florida. I'm 22-year-old extrovert who is outwardly confident (often times bordering on cocky), and I have started a successful career in sales. During college I ran a radio station, hosted events, had my own talk show, and was the radio voice of our football team. From that description you would probably assume I was born this way, a charismatic happy individual with a mouth that would never stop moving. Well, you would be sorely mistaken. In fact if you knew me ten years ago, you would think the exact opposite, that Patrick would be described as an undersized, nerdy kid with a serious anxiety disorder. Or even just a few years ago when I attempted suicide because I couldn't stand the sight of what I saw in the mirror anymore. So, if you will, take a step back with me, to that kid in Dinwiddie Virginia who had to run to the bathroom every day to burst into tears and couldn't explain why.

I was born into a military family with a mother and father who got married and moved to Germany after knowing each other for three weeks. My father is a military man turned federal prison employee, and my mom is a former business woman turned special education teacher. I have an older brother six years my elder with multiple learning disabilities. I went to four different elementary schools, and two different middle schools across four states and three regions. So, to say I had a "normal" childhood couldn't be any further from the truth. My parents and brother are the most wonderful people on planet earth, but my brother demanded a lot of attention at home, and my dad, the war veteran/federal prison employee, had enough on his plate to manage while trying to make enough money to give his family a life. My mother, god bless her soul, had to find a way to manage all of it and still put a hot dinner on the table every night. So, to me, my problems seemed like they would be a burden (in my own head) to them.

I was a happy young kid born in Colorado. After kindergarten I made a short stop in Pennsylvania, but when I moved to Virginia, things began to change. At 7 years old, I had to learn a hard lesson: cultures are different. I went from my lily-white world to an African American majority rural school in Virginia. I didn't fit in with anybody. It had nothing to do with the blackness of my classmates (as a matter of fact, if the roles were reversed, I think a black student would have faced worse problems). However, no one spoke like me, we didn't listen to the same music, my church was boring while their church was fun, my food sucked compared to theirs, our parents didn't idolize the same people, hell I didn't know who Martin Luther King Jr was until Black History Month rolled around my first year (you can imagine the reactions weren't great when I raised my hand asking who the most seminal figure of the Civil Rights Movement was to a black teacher raised in the Jim Crowe South). All I wanted was to fit in and have friends, and thankfully, I did make a few. That didn't change the fact that I was constantly looked at as different, and for seven-year-old Pat Broe, that meant constant panic attacks and deep-seated insecurities in my own identity.

I bounced around to another elementary school in the same town and then off too middle school. It took some time, but I actually gained a pretty large group of friends and a sense of community. Now, how I did this is exactly how you shouldn't. I created a false outward identity so that I could fit in. Instead of being me, I was someone else that would fit in. This is a great strategy during school hours, not so great when you go home and still hate the real you who no one understands. But just as I became relatively comfortable in my Virginia home, it was time to pick up and move again, this time Baraboo, Wisconsin.

This time the move was in the middle of my seventh-grade year. Nomads like me know that a mid-year move may be the worst of them all. Most students dread those first day ice breakers, but I needed them. I actually needed to introduce myself to my classmates. See, being the new kid is cool for about one day. Everyone is excited to meet you, but the kid who had gained a country accent pretty much immediately faced the same problems I had on my last move, but this time everything was so…white. It was freezing cold, and the snow was whiter than the people. I remember vividly almost getting kicked out of class my first week for calling my female teacher "mam" in class (I am pretty sure you can still hit children in Virginia if they don't call their elders sir or mam). But I knew what I needed to do; fake Pat #2 was created, and this time he was a jockey asshole.

Now I will say, jockey asshole Pat got by quite well, a golden child in fact. He made a lot of friends, and he was a "popular kid" through his high school career, but this constant lie about identity was just short of the prerequisites for true jockey assholedome (physically and esthetically). I am short, absurdly short for a man in fact, and this does not play well in jockey asshole land.

"Human Chode" was one of the nicknames I had in high school years denoting my short and stocky nature. Urban Dictionary defines a chode as "A fat **fucking dick**. A dick that is **wider** than it is long. A real **turn off** for the ladies". Now don't get me wrong, I did my fair share of teasing and ridiculing to fit into jockey assholedome (which I deeply regret), but for a kid who had no idea who he was, or why the Midwest was so different and the real him could never fit in, it was no help. Also, I had dealt with bullying before, like when Mathew Hum* told me in the fourth grade that he would come to my house and cut up my family if I didn't stop answering the teachers questions, but I could change that nerdiness. I couldn't change how tall I was. I fit in, but I never really fit in. I can't blame the Wisconsinites for never really getting me. All they knew was the fake me, and after all, they were just kids trying to find their way in this messed up world too.

High School was the culmination of my anxiety. I would be in class cracking jokes one minute and running to the bathroom to have a panic attack the next. Then I found a new solution; after having numerous ankle injuries through sports, I was prescribed hydrocodone, an opioid painkiller, and man did it kill the pain, not only in my ankle, but in my head too. The problem was that when the pills wore off, I would both mentally and physically feel worse than when I first popped the pill. Thus, the cycle began. It was the fall of my junior year and the opioid wear off was just too strong this time. I was home alone "sick" from school looking in the mirror looking at myself saying out loud, "I hate you, why are you this way, no wonder why no one likes you, no one should like you, you piece of shit, why don't you just die". Then I got an idea. Why didn't I just die? A fistful went down the hatch.

Now, medically, I am not sure why my body purged them five minutes later, and the vomiting literally exhausted me to the point of fainting, but I've never been so thankful for my weak stomach. I thankfully, did not die that day, but a lot of me did. Every fake Pat I had every known did. I awoke to a weird sense of peace, like god had given me a second chance.

See, there are a lot of things I didn't realize about the story I just told you until that very moment, that made me who I am today (or maybe I was the last one to find out). All those times I thought were painful were the greatest gifts I had ever received.

The moves, although stripping me of any sort of cultural identity, gave me a sense of empathy that none of my classmates had. This gave me the ability to understand almost anyone I talk to on a deeper level than almost anyone. Also, all those times having to start over with brand new friends gave me an ability to start a conversation with just about anyone. Maybe most of all, I have more cultural touch points than just about anyone, I've seen this nation from sea to shining sea and can find something to relate with anyone almost instantly.

I resented my father a lot as a child. After all it was his jobs that moved me around so much. He missed a lot of holidays and sometimes came home angry. But he taught me the value of hard work and humility. He didn't move us for spite; he moved us to give me a better future. Each move meant a pay raise which meant a better shot for his sons to be successful. He got up every day at 3:30 am, tied his literal boot straps, and headed to a place of work that we all fear just to put food on the table. Than man saw the horrors of war and has scars deeper than most of us will ever know, yet he is the kindest and strongest man I've ever met. Remember that the next time you get cut off on the highway.

My mother deserves every award on Earth. She had to manage a son with learning disabilities, a husband who was beat up physically and emotionally from his day, and me the wild child. She did this all with more grace and wisdom then I've ever seen. All while forcing *her children* to learn everything they possibly could, because she knew education would be our liberation. I cannot imagine balancing any of that. Thanks mom.

My brother had so much more to deal with then I did. Yet, his soul is so pure I'm pretty sure it hurts him emotionally to swat a fly. You think I had a lot to deal with moving so much, imagine everything that I dealt with and the classroom being a struggle as well despite behind those disabilities is the smartest man I have ever known.

I was so caught up in my own false identities to ever understand the people that did believe in me. There have been so many of you throughout the years who did see the real me under those fake identities. And for all of you, I am eternally grateful.

I haven't had a panic attack in 5 years. I talk for a living, and I have to say I'm pretty damn good at it. I have many relationships with people that I actually let know I appreciate, and they are all based in love. I am overtly myself. In fact, I probably annoy people with how loud and brash I am. So, if you've made it this far, embrace those shitty moments, don't run from them. They make you who you are, and I promise that you are beautiful just the way you are.

I wrote that article to tell my story. While I had personally felt past my darkest days (and had spent the better part of a half-decade working to do so), it felt as if I was living my last lie. There is much perceived shame cast on those of us who struggle with our mental health. In fact, there is shame cast to anyone who doesn't seem to be perfect. Not being upfront about my struggles added a layer of deceit to my internal shame. Being that is was the late 2010's, you couldn't go to any room without a Drake song playing, and a quote from "Take Care" loomed over my head:

"My only wish is I die real cause that truth hurts and those lies kill."

(I bet this is the only book you will read that will quote Drake, Dolly Parton, and Socrates). I had become the smiliest, happiest guy you could imagine (and it was real this time), working rooms someone of my social stature should never, yet it all felt like a lie.

I knew I had to do something to rectify this lie. Though I had thought about that day laying on the bathroom floor many times, I had never really taken a broad view of the story. In order to tell the truth, I had to know it in its totality. The best way I thought to do that was to just write it down. When I sat down to write, words left my body before I could type them. This was visceral, like every memory moved through my fingers. Forty-five minutes later, I had completely lived through my life, and it happened to show up on the page (I was sweating like a motherfucker by the way). When I read back through that out of body experience that appeared on the page, I then realized I would have to retell this story over and over again to everyone in my life I felt I was hiding this part of me from. Aside from being a logistical nightmare, having a reading from the book of Pat Broe to all my friends repeatedly sounded as fun as a tooth pulling. So I took what at this point was a Word document and sent it to some friends. After their initial reaction of "we had no idea", they all said, "Pat more people need to read this".

When weighing what I should do, I knew I would not be the only one implicated in telling my story. My world would surely have questions about going public with such sensitive information. I gathered my then-roommates and great friends around our kitchen table to ask their opinion. Additionally, I called others who were like family but didn't share my four walls. It should be noted I did not call my mom and dad, which I very much should have (talk to your parents more, they're awesome).

At this point I was a mild local celebrity, I ran my universities radio program, was the radio voice of the football program, was the host of a podcast for the college of business (which failed horribly), had a weekly talk show and was slated to be my graduations commencement speaker (which I did on Facebook live, fuck Covid). To top it all off, in mere months I would be stepping into a job that was on the list of Forbes toughest to get out of college where I would be talking to a new C-Level executive every day, all of which would Google me before an initial call. A Google search which would certainly populate an article like this. Despite these stakes, and the potential for everyone I knew to think I was a loon, my friends knew this article could do something great. As my friend Jarod stated, "this story could change people's lives". I did not have such delusions of grandeur, but with a deep breath and a swig of Mad Dog 20/20 (I was poor as shit; it was college ok), I clicked upload on my article and walked to my bedroom.

Little did I know that in a matter of hours, it would be shared thousands of times and seemingly every person I had ever interacted with would read it. I should have guessed with a provocative title like 'suicide to success" it would have made some traction, also the hubris to call myself successful before even starting my first full time job is hilarious.

Sitting in my dingey college bedroom on a bed taken from my grandparents' guest room, messages rushed into my social media inboxes. The responses were filled with love, respect, and thanks for telling my story. People I hadn't talked to since middle school, those who I talked to daily, and many I had never met before all felt obliged to reach out. Overwhelmed was the least of my emotions; a weight had been lifted from me, and it was doing good for the world? Yet, an unexpected sorrow washed over me as I sifted through the messages, a similar theme began to arise. *"Me Too."*

My 22-year-old naivete was not blind to the mental health crisis plaguing our youth and western society. I had seen the daily headlines of increased rates of suicide, and through my own healing process, I had been exposed to many stories like mine. What I didn't expect is how many people within an arm's distance were struggling my entire life. The news, and social media all give the illusion that statistics are not happening around us. Numbers on a screen aren't human. Political talking points are ways for politicians to one up their rivals, not a communication of the human experience. As our personalities have become commodities for our social media audience, we perceive everyone around us to be living shiny happy lives. That worldview came to a screeching halt for me as many of those shiny "happy" people shared their struggles with me. Having the great privilege of growing up across the country, and recently ending a nationwide internship, people reached out in places from Brooklyn to Bakersfeild. All of them shared their own struggles and asked me what I had done to get to where I am today. Then came my second realization, I had left one crucial detail out of my story. _How did I get better?_

When people asked me simply "how do I get better" or "what did you do?", I was at a loss for words. Silently this had been the focus of my life for a half decade, but the hard truth was there was no silver bullet answer. You can't get through an hour of TV without a *"stop the stigma"* message, which while nice, does nothing. I promise you no one going through the worst moment of their life is made happier because a celebrity on a TV advertisement tells people mental health is important. The extent of mental health messaging at this moment is essentially *"we see you, now go talk to a therapist that you definitely can't afford"*.

Not that I am cynical about people trying to stand up for mental health, but they can't tell you the truth, because that truth involves a hard journey. In working on myself, I had to shift through tons of garbage information, and none of it is built for modern youth. Turns out where there is a crisis, there are profiteers and snake oil salesmen with the newest remedy to save your life. Mental health is to the 2020's as physical health was to the 2000's (remember Weight Watchers, Curves, and every other diet fad moms tried) with charlatans whose profit depends on you not knowing any better. The modern mental health crisis's causation is entirely from modern sources, in a way that often is overlooked or misunderstood by our analog forefathers. However, when I gathered a semblance of the steps I took, it was immediately effective for the people I could share it with.

This book is that message of "how". *How did I get better, how can you get better*, and why you live in a world hell bent on fucking your brain. This book will set you on the path of becoming <u>The Real Confident You</u>. Real practical advice to improve your mental state in the modern world. Modern solutions to a modern problem. Don't take this as just for those struggling with mental health. The unique challenges of the modern world have its tentacles around all of us. We all have room for improvement. The lessons in this book are universal to us all. Hell, mental health struggles seem to be universal at this point. This book has three goals:

1. Help you recognize the unique challenges of the modern world and the damage they are causing you.

2. Give you the tools to live a happier more fulfilling life, improve constantly and become <u>"The Real Confident You"</u>.

3. How to help others do the same

As you probably are well aware, people in the self-help space tend to take themselves entirely too seriously. They take interesting subject matter and make it dryer than a Popeyes' biscuit you left in your backseat for a week. I will not be doing this. I am a deeply flawed human just like you. I am not your guru. People often grandstand about us young folk's mental health issues, but no one has told the story from our perspective. This is that perspective. Additionally, I very well recognize that I am showered in privilege (thankfully, I actually did develop a career worthy of that suicide to success title).

That said, I will try to make this as entertaining as possible while giving you tools that won't rob you blind via the American healthcare system or otherwise. That does not mean you will not be uncomfortable, however. This subject matter is hard, and the look I will be asking you to take in the mirror is even harder. Even so, you are not alone in this. Know that everything you're about to read, I have done, and failed at, many times. Also, I will never dare assert myself as an expert in neurochemistry, technology, sociobiology, or any other subject matter covered in this book. Rest assured those subject matters will be cited and given the proper credit to their proprietors. Furthermore, I will not be discussing any pharmaceutical medication in this book. This book will take that information and give it to you in a way that is consumable, with direct actions you can take in your life to finally find The Real Confident You.

Lastly, if you are contemplating taking your own life, please put this book down and dial this number.

1-800-273-8255

Prologue:

The Problem at Hand

***

"I suppose it is tempting, if the only tool you have is a hammer,
to treat everything as if it were a nail."
~ **Abraham Maslow, Toward a Psychology of Being**

What is the problem?

Buckle up, this is about to get grim.

The first step in solving any problem is understanding it. Your environment and how you engage with it is causing you many challenges. If you purchased this book, I am going to talk to you under the assumption that you are seeking answers on how you can build a happier and more fulfilled life. However severe your current situation is, you are far from alone. In fact, you are part of a growing majority (especially in our young people) that are struggling. The modern world is hellbent on destroying your brain, but it gives you no understanding of why and how to shield against it. It's not just mental health disorders. By all metrics we are becoming less happy, lonelier, and significantly less fulfilled in our lives. For those that struggle with their mental health, that kind of world is creating a dire situation.

Statistics often brush past us when a man in a suit is reading them off like a 3rd grade attendance report on the nightly news. The frames in which we view our society often indicate their impact on us. The problem we face is not nameless and faceless like indicated in the media; it lives in our homes, schools, workplaces, and churches.

* * *

The Data:

Neary **20% of high school students** have had serious thoughts of suicide. That means if you are teaching a high school class right now, 1 in 5 of your students has contemplated suicide deeply. Let's say you have graduated in the past decade. In your group chat, every 5th message is coming from someone who has contemplated ending their life.

There are many variables compounding the increase of mental health challenges for our youth, including social media. In the late 2010s, as social media became the dominant communication mechanism for teenagers and young adults, there began a sharp spike in depressive symptoms among that demographic. Specifically, the brunt of the negative mental health detriments felt by social media has affected young women. **Since the new millennium, adolescent depression rates have spiked by 60%,** with a much sharper increase for females who are more likely to use social media at high rates in their youth[1].

---

[1] Ivey, Asha Z. "Suicidal Ideation and Behaviors Among High School Students — Youth..." *CDC*, 21 August 2020, https://www.cdc.gov/mmwr/volumes/69/su/su6901a6.htm?s_cid=su6901a6_w. Accessed 7 January 2024.

Percent of U.S. high school students with high depressive symptoms, by sex[2]

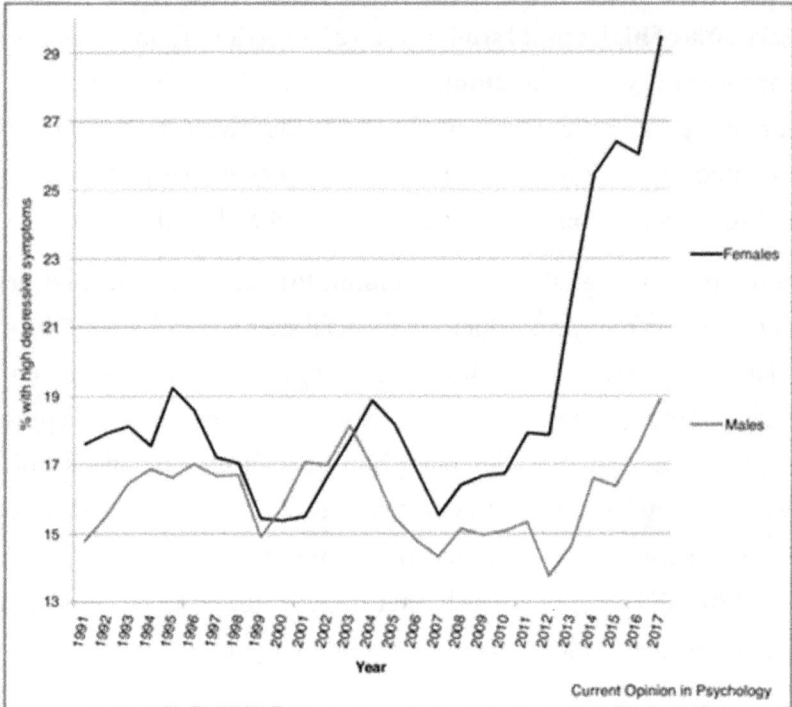

While social media seems to be a key contributor for both, this data would spell out that our current mental health crisis is not as severe of a problem for young men. That is not the case. Men are much more likely to go undiagnosed. Half of all suicide victims are undiagnosed[3]. Males are significantly more likely to commit suicide because of this reason.

[2] Sheffield, Rachel, and Catherine Francois. "Is Instagram Causing Poorer Mental Health Among Teen Girls? - Is Instagram Causing Poorer Mental Health Among Teen Girls? - United States Joint Economic Committee." *Joint Economic Committee*, 1 December 2021, https://www.jec.senate.gov/public/index.cfm/republicans/2021/12/is-instagram-causing-poorer-mental-health-among-teen-girls#_edn6. Accessed 7 January 2024.

[3] National Library of Medicine. "The Crisis in Male Mental Health: A Call to Action." *NCBI*, 7 July 2020, https://www.ncbi.nlm.nih.gov/pmc/articles/PMC7343362/. Accessed 7 January 2024.

83.6 percent of male successful suicides come from men without any previous diagnosis. The issue for young men is a growing concern, specifically by the National Library of Medicine[4] who states:

> *"Managing these emergent mental health issues in America's boys and men remains a significant challenge, as evidenced by the continual increase in truly tragic outcomes including addiction, depression, suicide, and violence. Many experts believe that the continued social and clinical problems that are well documented and continuing are related to several critical factors including the patterns of how and when boys and men access health care services, (and) how they perceive mental health."*

While much focus has been placed on the shocking upticks in poor mental health outcomes for our youth, it would seem that those of middle age and above remain unaffected. This is also not the case. As we progress in the digital age, technological adoption has become more widespread through middle aged and older generations. Subsequently, their effects on societal behavior and mental health detriments have spread. Greater than 1 in 5 adults would state their mental health as "poor", and many of them are unable to treat it with just more than 6 in 10 of those adults unaware of the care they need[5].

For adults, the issue of their own mental health has spilled into increased drug/alcohol abuse, prescription drug usage, or worse, homelessness and general destitution. Abuse numbers are also drastic, with 21.4 percent of adults claiming to have used an illicit substance or misused a prescription

---

[4] National Library of Medicine. "The Crisis in Male Mental Health: A Call to Action." *NCBI*, 7 July 2020, https://www.ncbi.nlm.nih.gov/pmc/articles/PMC7343362/. Accessed 7 January 2024.

[5] McPhillips, Deidre. "90% of US adults say the United States is experiencing a mental health crisis, CNN/KFF poll finds." *CNN*, 5 October 2022, https://www.cnn.com/2022/10/05/health/cnn-kff-mental-health-poll-wellness/index.html. Accessed 7 January 2024.

in the past year[6], and 17% of adults are binge drinkers[7]. More Americans are turning to the bottle than ever before, with the average American adult consuming an average of 603 drinks a year, as opposed to an average of 523 drinks in the late 1990s[8].

To make matters worse, the Covid-19 pandemic threw gasoline on the burning flame of this crisis. During the pandemic, anxiety and depression increased 25% worldwide[9]. Being shuttered into your home for months on end with nothing to do but look at your phone and watch *Tiger King* is detrimental to anyone's mental state. Throw in a pandemic to an already growing mental health crisis, and you have a recipe for societal disaster.

* * *

Our first takeaway should probably be that we need to start treating people better. However your reaction was probably similar to mine, *"We're fucked"*. Nevertheless, if you are struggling, understand you are far from alone. This is our scene. Now what can you do about it for yourself and your family?

Our environment is set to cause mass mental health issues. No one will argue it is harder now to live than in 1944. The problem is not weaker people; it's a new world filled with people who are unequipped to take on

---

[6] National Center for Drug Abuse Statistics. "Drug Abuse Statistics." *NCDAS: Substance Abuse and Addiction Statistics [2023]*, National Center for Drug Abuse Statistics, 2023, https://drugabusestatistics.org/. Accessed 7 January 2024.

[7] Centers for Disease Control. "Data on Excessive Drinking." *CDC*, 2023, https://www.cdc.gov/alcohol/data-stats.htm. Accessed 7 January 2024.

[8] Pew Research Center. "10 facts about Americans and alcohol as 'Dry January' begins." *Pew Research Center*, 3 January 2024, https://www.pewresearch.org/short-reads/2024/01/03/10-facts-about-americans-and-alcohol-as-dry-january-begins/. Accessed 7 January 2024.

[9] World Health Organization. "COVID-19 pandemic triggers 25% increase in prevalence of anxiety and depression worldwide." *World Health Organization (WHO)*, 2 March 2022, https://www.who.int/news/item/02-03-2022-covid-19-pandemic-triggers-25-increase-in-prevalence-of-anxiety-and-depression-worldwide. Accessed 7 January 2024.

their challenges. How could they be? No humans before those walking on earth now have faced the issues you currently face. Our issues are incredibly unique to our time. This book will show you those issues. <u>The good news is, there is a solution, and it exists within YOU.</u>

Your problems will not be solved by anyone but you. The information age has merely just begun. Change has never been this fast, and unless we are thrown into a stone age apocalypse, <u>it will never be this slow again</u>. The world will continue to progress with no regard for your mental health or happiness. The exploitation of your brain is at its dawn. Despite all of this, **you** can be **your** savior. All of the tools to make sure you are not only ok but living a thriving fulfilled life exist within YOU. Over the course of this book, you will be shown the tools to become <u>The Real Confident You</u>. A person that is able to tackle the unique challenges of modernity in an authentic way you can be proud of.

If you are really invested in pulling yourself into living a happy and fulfilled life, I cannot promise I have all of the answers. In fact, I have none of the answers for you, and beware of those that say they do. There are no simple answers, only paths to find them yourself. The answers exist within you; this book will help you find those answers and lead you on a path of self-transformation impenetrable to the ills of our society.

If you think upon turning this page you will enter a straight shot to personal salvation, throw this book away now (please don't leave me a bad amazon review; I'm trying to make a living here). I have no doubt you have been attempting to improve your mental state, no matter how dire. You just don't have the proper tools to transform.

If you have ever stepped foot in a gym, you have seen a myriad of people giving great effort doing things completely incorrectly. You've seen it, a middle-aged man, tank top on, desperately holding onto his youth. In this scenario let's call him Luke. All he wants is a semblance of the sick bod he was once so proud of that made his dear wife Sami tremble. The barbed wire tattoo on his arm sags a little more than it used to. Luke puts his earphones in and plays "Dr. Feelgood" by Motley Crue (it's Sami's favorite), then steps up to the rack, picks up some weights, and does the exercise that will finally make his sleeves tight. In a spectacular pageant of middle-aged desperation, Luke swings his hips attempting to bring weights from his waist to his shoulder doing what he thinks is a bicep curl. Everyone in the gym gives an awkward side eye at his flailing, grunting, and rolling sweat. Luke is working his ass off, but it does not matter, because Luke is using poor technique. No matter how many times he throws those weights up, his biceps will not grow.

Just like your body, your mental state requires work, but work that is done correctly. Luke's biceps and your brain will not get any better if you continue to work really hard at something that is not going to help at all (didn't think you would become Luke in this story did you?). Also, Luke is oblivious. Luke will go home to Sami blissfully ignorant of how little progress he really made. That was me, and it's more than likely you, desperately trying to get better but oblivious of how.

If you want big biceps or a better mental state, it will require you to work hard the correct way. Finding The Real Confident You should be difficult, anything in our lives that is worth achieving is. Luckily you will be given the right tools. The onus is on you to practice them. Much like any good discipline, once you've practiced enough, you can teach others, and that is the only solution to our problem. We have done a terrible thing in America telling people there are quick fixes to complex problems. I have no such quick fixes for you. There is a constellation of problems in the 2020's that require your effort to be unaffected by. I don't have a pill, but I do have a path.

Part 1:
The Inputs

Chapter 1:

Learn to Breathe

━━━━━━ ❧ ❧ ━━━━━━

"Fear is excitement without breath." ~ **Fritz Perls M.D.**

You need to calm down my friend. If there is one broad similarity of modern humans it is our attention spans have dwindled progressively by the day. We are unable to confront our own thoughts, and that fear leads us to our cell phones, video games, or TV to act as virtual pacifiers to fill our attention spans. This problem is so pervasive, TikTok influencers have shifted their content to show two videos at the same time because their audience is unable to focus on only one video (a video that is often less than a minute long I might add). This is especially true the younger demographics go. The constant need to fill our attention spans and avoid facing feelings or responsibilities is often driven by a desire to escape discomfort or boredom. In today's fast-paced world, there is a plethora of distractions readily available, from social media scrolling to binge-watching entertainment. These activities provide instant gratification and a temporary escape from reality, allowing us to avoid confronting difficult emotions or fulfilling obligations. However, this constant seeking of external stimuli creates a cycle of dependency, where the need for distraction becomes habitual, hindering personal growth and emotional resilience.

Therein lies the problem. A concept we will talk a lot about further on your path is that your brain is designed for an ancient world. Human evolution has not moved with the speed of humanities advances. Our brains are not designed to intake this level of stimulation. Your brain evolved with a world a million years ago in mind to see high levels of stimulation as dangerous. However, with social media, TV, video games, and a general increase in the world's pace, you are now being stimulated at high levels all day. This digital influx is further exacerbated by the internet's vastness, offering an overwhelming amount of content at our fingertips. Coupled with a fast-paced lifestyle that values multitasking and efficiency, urban environments filled with noise and crowds, and a consumer culture promoting constant consumption, it's no wonder we all experience heightened levels of sensory input. These factors collectively contribute to a sense of overwhelm, making it challenging to find moments of peace and quiet amidst the incessant stimulation. You are quite literally tricking your brain into thinking it's in as much danger as being chased by a saber tooth tiger from the time you wake up until the moment you fall asleep. This constant stimulation places your brain into reaction mode, which causes stress, anxiety, racing thoughts, unwarranted fear, and excessive worrying[10]. No one is able to properly handle their emotions when they are constantly in their most stressed mode.

Even worse, what we use to relax is actually causing us much more stress than we realize. The high stress thresholds we put ourselves through cause us to lose the ability to control our thoughts. When we feel our most vulnerable and upset, we return to the habits (phone, tv, video games) that are actually triggering most of our anxious and depressed responses. Looking at your phone when you are stressed is like drinking Jack Daniels to get less drunk. These overstimulated behaviors peaked in the pandemic, while everyone was glued to the news and their phones during lockdowns. Remember how aggressive everyone was at the grocery store? That was an overstimulation response. *So if the problem is we are OVERstimulated how do we DEstimulate?*

---

[10] Peterson, Tanya J. "Overstimulation Causes Anxiety; How to Refocus and Feel Calm." *HealthyPlace*, 12 March 2020, https://www.healthyplace.com/blogs/anxiety-schmanxiety/2020/3/overstimulation-causes-anxiety-how-to-refocus-and-feel-calm. Accessed 9 January 2024.

Now if you read that and thought, *"Sure I could see how that's a problem, but it definitely does not apply to me"*, I have some bad news for you. Below are some telltale habits of overstimulated people. If any of these apply to you, there may be a problem:

1. Do you watch TV as background noise while you play on your phone?

2. Do you work or do homework with music playing to help you "focus" (this actually hurts your ability to focus btw)?

3. Do you need a podcast, tv, music, white noise, etc. to fall asleep?

4. Do you need to have music playing while you are in the shower?

5. Can you eat without TV, YouTube, music, or any social media when you're alone?

6. Can you make it through an episode of TV without checking your phone?

7. Have you sat in silence comfortably, with no technology usage, for more than twenty minutes in the past month?

8. When people talk to you, do you lose focus after a certain time?

9. Do you sleep less than 8 hours regularly?

10. You realize your phone isn't near you, do you freak out?

11. Is the last thing you look at before you fall asleep a screen?

12. Are you checking your phone within the first fifteen minutes of waking up?

13. Do you sleep next to your phone? (Do you sleep with the phone in bed?)

14. Can you work out without looking at your phone for any other reason than skipping a song? (Still don't know why I put Nikki Minaj on that playlist.)

15. Do you check your phone when you're driving?

16. Can you get through a chapter of a book uninterrupted?

17. Can you stand in a line, or in a public place with strangers, without being glued to your phone?

18. Can you do household chores without music or TV?

19. Do you experience mood swings?

20. Can you concentrate on work for more than a few minutes?

21. Have you checked your phone during this chapter?

22. Do you clinch your jaw?

23. Do you have routine digestive issues?

24. Do you feel tired often?

25. Would you describe yourself as "impulsive"?

26. Are you easily agitated?

27. Do you experience high anger daily?

28. Do you need caffeine to get through daily tasks?

29. Do your eyes hurt?

30. Could your posture be described as "slouched"?

31. Do you have mid-back pain?

32. Is there something you are procrastinating on right now?

33. Do you impulse buy?

If any of these apply to you, congrats, you are probably overstimulated (a lot of these apply to me too, like I've mentioned, deeply flawed but working on it). Notice, a lot of those have to do with your ability to hold attention and our discomfort when we aren't being stimulated. We will discuss how your brain's reward systems work later, but your brain is blissfully unaware that the things that give it "feel good chemicals" are also causing you immense stress.

Additionally, social media is designed specifically to be addictive. Social media platforms often employ techniques like notifications, rewards, and personalized content to create a sense of novelty and excitement, triggering dopamine release in the brain, which reinforces the behavior. Additionally, the convenience and accessibility of screens make it easy to turn to them for entertainment, information, and social interaction, leading to habitual use. Over time, this results in a reliance on screens for emotional regulation, social connection, and boredom relief, making it challenging to reduce screen time and break the cycle of addiction. Like any addictive substance, you aren't really choosing to do the addictive behavior. Have you ever picked up you phone and started scrolling only to look up fifteen minutes later thinking, *"What the fuck am I doing?"*.

So we are overstimulated which causes us stress, but because we are junkies, we try to comfort that stress with something that makes us more stressed out? Seems like a problem. I wish I could now lead you to your Amazon cart where you could find a magic destimulation pill, but big pharma is more concerned with Ozempic at the moment. However there is a manual way for us to destimulate, and it takes surprisingly little effort. We have to breathe.

We are going to walk through a breathing exercise. I know what you're thinking, here comes the fucking hippie trying to solve all my problems with a yoga retreat. I am well aware that when most people think of breathing exercises they imagine a man with a long beard with a group of white people who shop at Trader Joes and reek of 'natural' deodorant chanting "hom" in a dimly lit room. However, what I am about to show you is a technique used by navy seals, elite athletes, dancers, actors, and artists alike. This technique is used to calm elite performers down in their most tense moments, to slow heartbeat, decrease blood pressure, and lower anxiety. You will be doing it to yank yourself out of your reactionary state. It's like hitting the reset button on all that built up stimulation. You are getting your hands back on the wheel of a car that is out of control. When I started using this technique, it stopped my panic attacks in their tracks. When I integrated it into my daily life, I became less defensive, calmer, and first began to find the clearest thoughts of my true self without negative interruption. Navy Seal Mark Divine said it best when describing this technique. *"When I perform box breathing even just for five minutes, I am left with a deeply calm body and an alert, focused state of mind.[11]"*

The technique we are going to do is commonly known as "box breathing". You probably have done something similar in the past. However, I have added an additional layer in my practice that helped me take control of my own thoughts. If you are listening to this on audiobook and driving, or not in a place where you can be alone with your thoughts, please close this book and come back when you are. If you can, you are going to do this technique for the first time now.

Box Breathing for Sensory Reset Part 1

Step 1: Pull out the notes app on your phone or a notepad nearby and write the date, a line that says "Intention:", and a second line that says "Feeling:"

Step 2: Set an intention for why you picked up this book today. This can be anything, but think about it and be honest with yourself about what you are looking for. Then write that down next to the word "Intention:". Second, take a check on yourself. How would you describe your feelings today? Write down a word or two describing your feelings next to "Feeling:'.

Step 3. Sit upright, place your hand on your stomach and begin breathing into your stomach. If you are breathing deeply, you should feel your stomach rise and fall. Purposely move the flow of air to your stomach and away from your upper chest.

---

[11] Divine, Mark. "Breathing Technique for Calm: Tips from a Navy Seal." *Time*, 4 May 2016, https://time.com/4316151/breathing-technique-navy-seal-calm-focused/. Accessed 9 January 2024.

Step 4: You are now going to close your eyes and begin to box breath (not yet obviously, read how to do it). With your hand on your stomach and eyes closed you will:

Inhale for four seconds (through nose, mouth shut).

Hold your breath for four seconds.

Exhale for four seconds (through nose, mouth shut).

Hold your breath for four seconds.

Repeat the cycle 10 times or set a timer for three minutes if you're scared of losing count.

These inhales should be deep, stretching your stomach like a balloon. Don't cheat any breaths either. Go right into your holds and exhales for the full cycle. In your head all you will be doing is counting. The cadence should sound something like *Inhale, one..two..three.. four, Hold, one…two..three..four…*

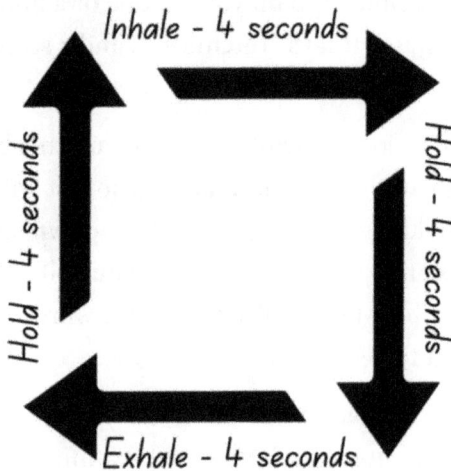

Inhale - 4 seconds

Hold - 4 seconds

Hold - 4 seconds

Exhale - 4 seconds

Now, start this exercise. Do not read ahead until you have completed it ten times or for three minutes.

Welcome back and congratulations! You have just successfully reset your nervous system. Now let's revisit your notes app and finish the exercise.

Box Breathing for Sensory Reset Part 2

Step 5: Revisit your notes app or notebook and write two new lines that say "Destimulated Emotion:" and "Gratitude:"

Step 6: Finally, next to "Destimulated Emotion:", write how you are feeling after the exercise. This may not be a positive emotion, but it should be different. Then, next to "Gratitude:" pick one thing you are thankful for.

Step 7: If you feel no change, start the exercise again, this time for four minutes.

You know how you feel right now? That's how you are supposed to feel all of the time.

We are now brain training. Much like a weight in the gym, your thoughts are the tool that you can use to shape the patterns and strength of your brain. Like Luke, who was probably doing more damage to his body than benefit, you need to learn how to use the muscle between your ears. You have no control of your brain when it's overstimulated, so by box breathing, we allow our bodies to leave a reactionary state and enter a place where your conscious mind is in total control. Setting an intention allows our brain to use the parts of it that will give us the outcomes we are looking for. Understanding our feelings and how we are able to manipulate them with our actions gives us a better understanding of when we are overstimulated.

Also, it gives you practice shifting your emotions, helping you control your mind. Your brain is a car, you just need to learn how to drive it. By using this exercise, you give your brain intentional reps in transforming your emotional state and entering a clear intentional zone. When we repeat these kinds of exercises over a long period, we can transform our thoughts and ultimately behaviors to be under our control, and our unconscious behaviors will follow suit. Thus, we can recognize when our patterns have gone array and know exactly how to get on the right path.

Did You Know? Neuroplasticity

"Any man could, if he were so inclined, be the sculptor of his own brain." ~ **Santiago Ramon**

Big word alert. If your brain is constantly changing, you better be a part of that change. Neuroplasticity refers to your brain's ability to change and reorganize itself. Most people live their lives with the perception that their personalities, disposition, and abilities come from birth and last forever. This is simply not true. Your brain has an incredible ability to adapt and change.

Take Gabrielle Giffords, a congresswoman from Arizona who in 2011 was shot in the head during close range in an assassination attempt. Aside from the pure miracle of her survival, Gabbie had a large uphill battle to climb. She had sustained injuries to her Broca's Area, the region in our brain which allows us to form speech, meaning while she could understand the world around her, including what people were saying, she was completely unable to form a sentence. A woman who had made a career with impassioned communication could now no longer speak. Her doctors, however, came to a brilliant conclusion: music doesn't use exclusively the Brocas Area. Because her brain was not damaged in many of the more complex areas our brain uses for music, she was slowly able to use singing to build new pathways for speech in her. The woman who couldn't speak could still sing. With

---

the power of neuroplasticity and training through music, she was able to back-engineer how to speak again. Almost a decade later, Gabbie is a force of hope to those who have sustained major injuries. Through her own brain's ability to adapt, brilliant doctors, and a little music, she speaks with passion once again.

Not only is that an awesome fucking story, it's an example of how your brain is much more malleable than you believe. Your behaviors, emotions, and ability to grow are all able to change depending on your inputs.

Like a dysfunctional relationship, these negative thoughts have become your home. Many of us are scared that if we change our current state, we will not keep the things about ourselves we like. It's scary to face change, especially when we don't trust ourselves to get to the other side. If anyone said to us the things we say to ourselves, they would be our mortal enemies. Change also seems isolating; no one could ever understand what you are going through. The truth you need to face is you are going to change whether you take part in that change or not. You are not a tree in the ground rather a ship in a vast ocean, are you going to steer that ship or put your head in your phone and let the ship guide you. You have two options:

1. Take control of your own change by destimulating, learning your own brain and guiding it the way you want.

   or

2. Continue down the path you are on now.

If you chose option one, turn the page.

Chapter 2:

Your Mind as a Muscle

------- ✤✤ -------

"It is the mark of an educated mind to be able to entertain a thought without accepting it" ~ **Aristotle**

Any self-respecting gym try hard, or your friend who sells Herbalife on Facebook, can tell you all of the basic muscle groups of the human body. People make millions of dollars a year telling you the one exercise that will finally make your ass look like Kim Kardashians or biceps look like Ronnie Colemans (both of which are chemically enhanced). In your middle school health class, you learned the basic muscles of the human body and what they do. Yet there is almost no common knowledge of how your brain works. Sure you learned that men's frontal lobes form later than women's and have been saying it at parties to describe why guys are immature, but you have no idea what a frontal lobe does. Maybe that's a little harsh. Nevertheless, most of us walk around completely ignorant to the wrinkly thing in our skull.

I am well aware the last thing you wanted to do is open an anatomy textbook today. Truthfully, much of the brain is still a mystery to modern science. That science is also continuously changing (that's the case for the body too, remember when the food pyramid told us to eat 60% of our diet in bread?). However, this chapter will take on some of the mechanisms of your brain, how they cause you to perceive the world, and what may be standing in the way of finding your true self. Unlike the food pyramid, everything presented will be as concrete as I can find, and it has a direct correlation to our modern problem. Additionally, if you are an expert in the human brain, I can feel your eye rolls already.

The Prehistoric Problem

I will be treating evolution as a fact in this book. For the religious extremist crowd, please do not show up at my house with signs that say, "God Hates Broe". Just throw away the book, and again, leave Amazon reviews alone. I'm trying to make a living here.

300,000 years ago, humanity started. Apes stood on two feet with a loin cloth, started chanting some unga bungas, and became your first relatives. Those distant relatives set off to become the most powerful species this planet has ever seen. They were able to succeed (after a couple hundred thousand years of trials and tribulations, read *Sapiens* by Yuval Noah Harari) because they were perfectly designed to dominate the world they lived in. A couple of ice ages, global famines, pandemics, plagues, Aeropostale t-shirts, natural disasters, and economic collapses weren't enough to stop the progress of our species. Innovation by innovation, your relatives went from running away from lions all day to landing on the moon.

Every generation brought a new invention that transformed the human experience. While your ancestors geared this world to convenience, humans have trouble seeing past innovations' short-term benefits and seeing their long-term flaws. Henry Ford didn't see his cars causing a global climate crisis, Eli Whitney did not see the cotton gin exploding the slave trade, and Mark Zuckerburg did not see Facebook turning our brains to mush. With our successes, one of the most undeniable truths of humanity is our inability to see the challenges our innovations will cause us. The challenge of today we face today is another ill of our innovations. Our world evolved faster than our brains could evolve with it.

You have the same amount of computing power it took NASA to get to the moon in your phone; that's fucking nuts. While the smartphone, internet, and social media have made all of our lives incredibly easier, it also has created quite the conundrum for our brain. You have a brain built for a much simpler world. The amount of technology we interface on a daily basis is not just overwhelming for your monkey brain, but it makes a reality indiscernible. In 2020, Tristan Harris released a documentary on Netflix titled *"The Social Dilemma"*. Tristan is a former technologist at Google. He realized the company not only knew they were causing mass harm to society but refused to do anything about it. His documentary details how social media's success is dependent on how well an app can "hack" your brain. In short, social media companies make money from ads. The more ads you view, the more money they make. To get you to view more ads, they need you to be on the app as long as possible, and to do this, they have programmed social media to hijack your prehistoric brain to make it nearly impossible to look away.

Social media companies make money by selling your attention to advertisers. <u>You are the product.</u> Ever wondered why you sit down thinking you'll spend a couple minutes clearing notifications and you've looked up and it's an hour later and you have no idea how? Your brain was not designed for this much stimulus. In fact, it treats it much like a drug. The Addition Center conducted a study which found social media has a similar effect on the brain as Opioids, Meth, and Cocaine[12].

I am not saying you're a crackhead. What I am saying is this technology was made with the knowledge that it will absolutely ruin your mental health. Can you handle it? Sure, but like a flip phone trying to load a YouTube video. Your ancient hardware is not designed for modern hardware. If you handed a caveman your iPhone, I am fully confident they would burst into flames. That said, if Mark Zukerburg can hack your brain, so can you. Let's continue and get to know that muscle in your head a little bit.

---

[12] Addiction Center. "Social Media Addiction", 9 November 2017, https://www.addictioncenter.com/drugs/social-media-addiction/. Accessed 3 February 2024.

Dunbar's Number

Have you ever felt guilty about going back to your hometown and forgetting someone's name when you run into them at the grocery store? You shouldn't. Did you know you can only remember 150 people at a time?

Dunbar's number, proposed by anthropologist Robin Dunbar, represents the limit on relationships that humans can maintain, estimated at around 150 individuals. Our brain's capacity for social interaction is constrained by its cognitive processing abilities. Essentially your brain only has so much storage for people. Within this framework, relationships are organized into layers or circles, with the innermost circle comprising close friends and family members (around 5-15 people) with whom individuals share strong emotional bonds and frequent interactions. The next circle expands to include acquaintances and extended family (15-50 people), followed by a wider social circle (50-150 people) consisting of a broader network of friends, colleagues, and community members. When you forget that guy from little league, it's not a big deal.

The Conscious vs. Subconscious Mind

The average person operates their life as if every decision they make is rational. As if you weigh buying gum with the importance of picking a career. Your brain does not work like that. Would you be shocked that 90% of the decisions you make in a day you don't actually think about[13]? Would it surprise you even more to find out that most of what you do in a day is controlled by the part of your brain that uses as much thinking power as a lizard? Simplistically, your brain is split into two parts: the

---

[13] Lamartine, Alphonse. "95 Percent Of Our Decisions Are Made By Our Unconscious Mind." *The Minds Journal*, 15 August 2023, https://themindsjournal.com/quotes/95-percent-of-our-decisions-are-made-by-our-unconscious-mind/. Accessed 9 January 2024.

part that we have inherited from our animal ancestors, and the part that makes us human. Our animal brain is in control of most of our day-to-day functions: pain, hunger, when you have to pee, your long term memory, long term habit forming, pattern recognition, and most of your emotions are all controlled by this part of your brain. When you wake up and walk to the sink to brush your teeth you don't even think about it, simply it just happens.

This instinctual animal part of our brain is our subconscious mind. The part of your brain that makes you a human is your ability to think or your conscious mind (some more than others). All of the pink wrinkly mess that we associate with the brain is a byproduct of human evolution. When we encounter something new in the world, our human brain notices and stores it in our memory. Our memories come from patterns, and this is where your animal brain takes back over. You brush your teeth without thinking because your mom made you do it every night. For thousands of years, being a human on this planet was dependent on our ability to think quickly. When a tiger is jumping at you, there is no time to think, "I need to run away", you just run away.

This shortcut our subconscious mind uses is the main mechanism we use today. As we operate through life, you are faced with thousands of decisions. Your primal brain creates shortcuts to functions, so you don't spend all day telling yourself to lift up the water and put it in your mouth. This primal part of your brain is in control of your subconscious, which in theory is great. Who wouldn't love to save a little time on how much they think?

However, your subconscious sucks. It has no ability to use reason, logic, or anything we would associate with a human thought. These reactionary mechanisms control most of your day-to-day life and are simply outdated to cope with the modern world. While your rational conscious brain is perfectly capable of seeing a mean comment on Instagram, rationalizing it, and moving on with your day, not letting it affect you, your subconscious will respond based on patterns.

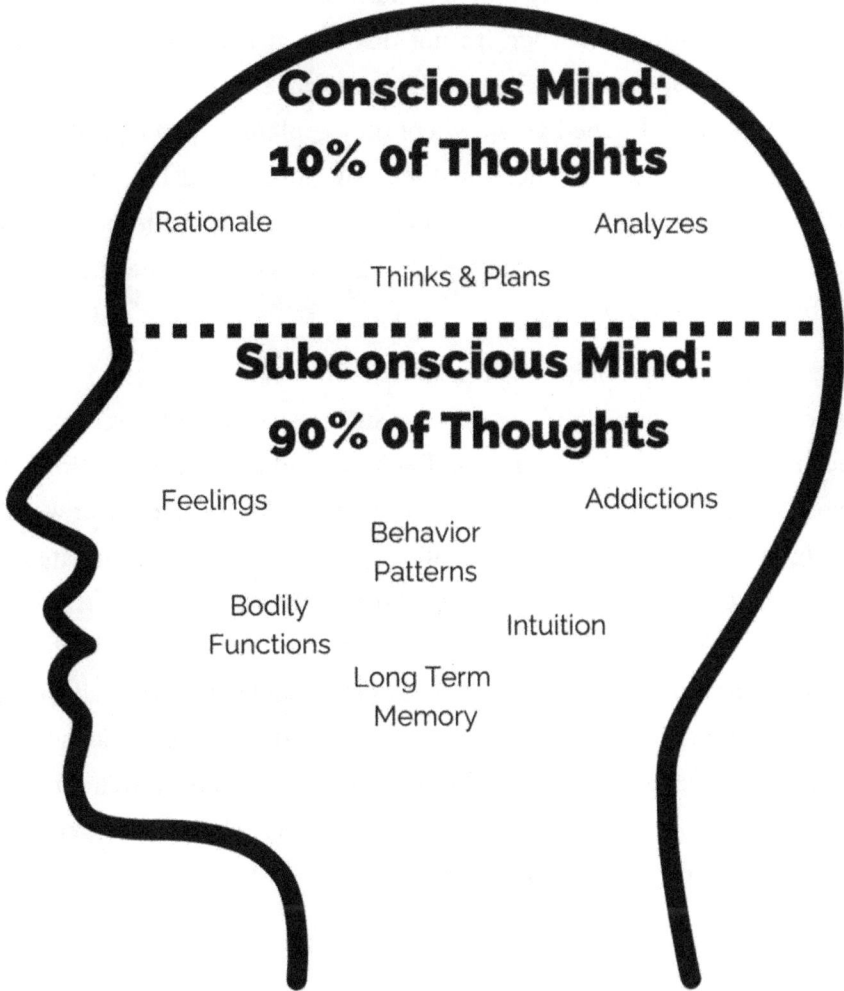

Conscious Mind: 10% of Thoughts

Rationale   Analyzes

Thinks & Plans

Subconscious Mind: 90% of Thoughts

Feelings   Addictions

Behavior Patterns

Bodily Functions   Intuition

Long Term Memory

Your subconscious is a sponge. It's there to notice things you are not conscious of at all. Have you ever noticed how little kids seem to absorb the entire world around them? Their subconscious is a blank slate. Not only do they not have deep seated patterns built, they are also absorbing the entire world even when it's not directed at them. Marketers have known this for decades. This is why most advertisements work. How often have you watched an ad where they explain to you logically why you should buy something, and then you go out and buy that item? Probably never. If there was a pitchman selling you the benefits of McDonalds, you would never visit the golden arches. Instead they use subliminal messaging.

If Micheal Jordan holds a Big Mac next to his head, a marketer in a high rise in Manhattan is banking on your subconscious tying your positive feelings of Micheal Jordan to that Big Mac (and it works every time). If your conscious mind were to lay out a trip to McDonalds, you would weigh its benefits (it's delicious and fast) to its drawbacks (its inflated in price, it probably is slowly killing you, you will feel terrible fifteen minutes after and probably for the rest of the day), and you would choose whether or not to go. But that is not how our brain works. Instead we are tired, driving home from a long day at work and our subconscious brain sees the McDonalds logo and tells us "cheeseburger good". An hour later we are at home, we feel like shit, and have no idea why we just spent $20 on a paper bag of delicious cancer.

Lights, Camera, Pepsi?

No one knows more about how to hack your subconscious brain like the movies. Did you know most blockbuster movies are heavily funded by product placements? Take for instance the Marvel universe. Now, there has never been a scene as explicit as Captain America drinking a Pepsi and saying a line like, "Damn this Pepsi was delicious, it's really going to help me save the world". What movie makers do is place products all over the screen so that your subconscious brain will notice.

Have you ever noticed that all of the big fight scenes in Marvel movies take place in a big city center? I always wondered why Hulk couldn't just smash a guy in a field in Ohio so no bystanders would get hurt. Writers do this so they can fill the screen with ads to sell. As Ironman soars through Times Square fighting his newest bad guy, he is passing numerous ads that Disney has sold and advertisers know your subconscious will pick up on. Someone driving in a car on screen? The car company paid for that car to be there. Someone eating at a chain restaurant? The chain paid for that. Often entire wardrobes will be paid promotion deals because Banana Republic is banking on you tying the good feeling you have about a movie back to their Chino Pants. It's not just Marvel; in 2022, **$22.3 billion** was spent on such movie tie-ins, with an expected 13.9% increase in 2023[14].

In 2011, Morgan Spurlock of *Super Size Me* fame made a documentary about how pervasive subliminal advertising in movies had become titled *POM Wonderful Presents: The Greatest Movie Ever Sold*. In the film, he demonstrated how movies are made through ad sales by

---

[14] Marketing Interactive. "Did you spot these 5 brand cameos in Marvel films?" *Marketing-Interactive*, 13 May 2022, https://www.marketing-interactive.com/did-you-spot-these-5-brand-cameos-in-marvel-films. Accessed 3 February 2024.

selling ads in his movie about ad sales. The film is a combination of showing the film funding process while also pointing out what you have missed in your viewership up to this point. For instance, did you know what's on the shelves in the background of sitcoms changes? In a rerun episode of King of Queens aired on TBS, the background had been digitally altered to have a DVD copy of "How to Train Your Dragon" on a living room shelf. The TV episode was filmed in 2003, "How to Train Your Dragon" came out in 2010. Some film exec bought advertising space on an old episode of TV in a place you wouldn't even notice because they knew your subconscious would. Aside from *The Greatest Movie Ever Sold* being a brilliant film, Morgan actually is able to sell all of the ads in his film. Advertisers understood that even in a movie exposing how advertising has ruined movies, their ads in this movie would still work because your subconscious mind will still see their brands. Kind of insidious if you ask me.

So how do we fix this? Well you have thankfully already started by acknowledging the stimulation problem. Remember, when our conscious mind is fully preoccupied, all we have is our subconscious. Additionally, just knowing is half the battle. I am not Sigmund Frued or your therapist, but it's safe to say most of the habits of thinking you've picked up are from your childhood. Your subconscious is easily penetrable as seen through marketing, but the things that we do consistently over time are what really make it tick. Like water, we will always move in the path of least resistance. Whatever grooves have been worn in over time is often what you'll do, because your subconscious is looking for the shortcuts you need to get through the day.

The negative feelings in life become our default mode, because that's what's easiest for our mind to understand. We find a certain safety in being the way we currently are because we know it so well. What I am asking of you, and what you need to ask of yourself, will take some courage. What grooves are deep inside of you that you refuse to let go? Are you angry because *"That's just who I am"*, or are you not acknowledging that something needs to change? Do you really not know why you're sad, or is it just uncomfortable to try happiness? While your subconscious is reactionary, it's still you. You are the one making the decision on what to feed it. It will only react based on the stimulus you input, so what are your feeding your brain?

The Power of Mind Orientation

If I asked you how many red cars you passed on the way home from the gas station, could you tell me? You can't. Now what if I told you to make the same trip, but this time, I will give you $1000 for every red car you see. I'd venture to say you would remember every red car.

When we point our brain at our lives, what we look for is often what we find. You simply are unable to pay attention to everything consciously at once, but when we position our mind for what we are looking for, we can find it easily. I get that this sounds silly, but it's your choice what you do and don't pay attention to. What you pay attention to, without even realizing it, is absorbed more by your subconscious mind than what's going on in the background.

With our limited brain capacity, if we don't control where we orient our attention we allow unwanted stimuli to affect us. Back to the breathing exercise this is why setting the "intention" is so pivotal. Your brain has limited space and needs direction in order to be used the way you want it. When we provide this direction repeatedly, the orientation decisions we make become subconscious habits, and this will change how you take in the world in the long term. You have to form your own grooves for the water to pass through. Most people would refer to this as their "disposition". You'll often hear people describe traits like "optimistic" or "pessimistic" as if it were a trait they were born with. Truthfully, this is a result of their repeated orientation, probably based on what they witnessed or was reinforced by their parents. Because we have neuroplasticity, if we push our thoughts in the direction we want them to go, soon our mood, disposition, and life will follow. For us to stop our own self destruction, we must actively position ourselves to what we truly want.

University of Bath Study

The University of Bath is a research university in the U.K., not a place where bathing is studied. In 2001 they ran a study to see how mental orientation played a role in building better exercise habits. The subjects examined were split into three groups:

Group 1: "Control Group" - Subjects were asked to track how much they exercised.

Group 2: "Motivation Group" - Researchers asked them to read about the benefits of exercise and also track frequency of exercise.

Group 3: "Intention Group" - not only tracked their exercise frequency and read material on the benefits of exercise, but they were also asked to create a specific plan outlining when and where they would workout. Their plan would follow a specific format: "During the next week, I will partake in at least 20 minutes of exercise on [DAY] at [TIME] in [PLACE].

The third group moved with intention, forcing them to orient their thoughts to the outcomes they desired. They had to think out a plan for how they were going to work out. This meant they not only had to absorb the material but position their brain to imagine themselves not in the end state, but in the process of getting healthy.

The results were astonishing:

Group 1: 35% of people exercised at least once a week.

Group 2: 38% of people exercised at least once a week.

Group 3: 91% of people exercised at least once a week.

Creating a plan is a great way to force our minds to orient to something. You can learn as much as you want about a subject, but until you focus on how you would tackle it, your mind doesn't put itself in those scenarios. Making a plan forces you to push your thoughts in the direction of what you want. A goal without a plan is a dream. Making a plan for your betterment is a great way to reach the goals you've been searching for in your journey[15].

In 2006 Rhonda Byrne released her bestselling book *"The Secret "* and it's garbage. In summary, she claims that there is a "law of attraction" and if you think about something hard enough, it will magically appear in your life. Despite that being an utter crock of nonsense, this book sold like hotcakes *(30 million copies)*. It was featured on Oprah's Book Club (for my Gen-Z friends, Oprah endorsing you in the 2000s would be equivalent to Taylor Swift endorsing it today) and sprung trends like vision boards and housewives repeating nightly manifestations.

While there is no law of attraction (boy I wish there was, because I would be on a beach with Margot Robbie and not writing this book), many people did see changes in their life. Why is that? Unfortunately Rhonda's readers did not imagine a Porche into existence. Inadvertently, "The Secret " led people to orient their thoughts to the things and feelings they actually wanted. The things they wanted didn't appear by some law of

---

[15] Tarver, Jordan. "The Power of Intention: How Daily Intentions Can Change Your Life." *Jordan Tarver*, https://www.jordantarver.com/the-power-of-intention. Accessed 3 February 2024.

attraction, rather they noticed what had been in front of them the whole time. Only now they have oriented their mind to what they want. Similarly with your personal growth, you can wish upon a star or a Prozac all you want, nothing will change until you direct your mind to the outcomes you want. Manifestation does work but not in a wu-wu hippie bullshit way. It works because your brain will only work the way you direct it. Like the red car, when you are intentionally looking for the things in life that make it better, you will find them more easily.

Have I gone to existential? Let me reel it in. The way you are feeling is due to what you focus on. I will not begin to understand the complexities of the experience that brought you to this book. The depth of your story is not limited to what you think. However, you do have control of what you see. You can dwell on the past, but it's your choice what to dwell on. From this moment forward, how you point your mind is something you own. Take pride in that control. If you find that kind of control hard to manage, let's practice how to not only control your mind but orient it where you want it to be.

Exercise: Perspective Shifting

Take out your notes app or a notepad.

Think about your day, write down 5 things that made you upset and write them down.

What emotion are you feeling? Write down one word to describe it. **Do this and don't read ahead.**

Think about your day again, this time, write down 10 things you are grateful for in your day.

Now what emotion are you feeling? Write down one word to describe it.

See how easy that was. Just by choosing what to focus on, you were able to change your entire mood. Now, I'd imagine it was much harder to find the things that you were grateful for, but that's ok! You haven't practiced it nearly as much as you have negative thoughts. Keep practicing and it will become easier. I used to be a real cynical son of a bitch, but over time I was able to work my brain hard enough to become only a partially cynical son of a bitch (kidding, kinda). What I can assure that was true for me will be true for you, if you intentionally take the time to check in on how you are oriented to the world, you will find being a human to be a much more exciting and beautiful experience. With practice and time, your life is full of only the things that make you the happiest.

Here is the hardest part of all. What are you looking for? I'm not asking you to chart your life's path here. Would you like to be happier? Do you have a negative self-image? Do you have a bad relationship with food? I can't choose where you point that arrow, but I can assure you where you point it, your life will follow.

Roses Really Smell Like Poo-Poo

In the 2000s the reality TV phenomenon flooded American airwaves. With it came The Discovery Channels mega hit "Dirty Jobs". Host Mike Rowe would spend each episode chronically a "dirty job" each week highlighting those of us that go thankless doing horrific jobs to keep our society afloat. Jobs like oil field workers, sewer inspectors, avian vomitologists (bird puke collector), and dairy cow inseminators. One of the unintended consequences of the show is that Mike found these people to be some of the happiest alive. In Mike's Ted Talk "Learning from Dirty Jobs[16]", he stated about the show:

---

[16] TED. "Mike Rowe: Learning from dirty jobs." *TED*, 4 March 2009, https://www.ted.com/talks/mike_rowe_learning_from_dirty_jobs. Accessed 3 February 2024.

"People with dirty jobs are happier than you think. As a group, they're the happiest people I know. And I don't want to start whistling "Look for the Union Label," and all that happy-worker crap. I'm just telling you that these are balanced people who do unthinkable work. Roadkill picker-uppers whistle while they work, I swear to God — I did it with them. They've got this amazing sort of symmetry to their life."

The people working these 'dirty' jobs days are filled with nothing but shit (some literally). So how on Earth are they so happy? Because they don't focus on the shit. What Mike found was that the majority of these focus took pride in what they did. They focused on that pride. The pride of feeding their family, the pride of serving their fellow man, and the pride of doing something really hard that others aren't willing to do. A roadkill picker upper could easily focus on the fact they're spending his days with dead racoons. Instead they orient their mind in a direction that makes them happy. So when you say "work sucks" or "school sucks", does it? Maybe you just need to shift your orientation.

Chapter 3:

Garbage In - Garbage Out

"They serve up distractions and we eat um' with fries, until the bomb falls out of our fucking sky." ~ **Sturgill Simpson**

In America, your job above all else is to consume. Shortly after the 9/11 attacks, then-President George W. Bush urged Americans that the most patriotic thing they could do is to shop:

> *"Our financial institutions remain strong. The American economy is still open for business...get down to Disney World in Florida, take your families and enjoy life the way we want it to be enjoyed."*

Now I get that part of ole President Dubbya's message was Americans shouldn't live in fear and return to their normal lives, but there is the problem. Most of our "normal lives" are just consuming things. I am not just talking about food. Media, cars, gasoline, clothes, shoes, the list is endless. We work jobs that mostly facilitate making something to be consumed, so we can have more money to spend on consuming things. Now, I am not going on some anti-capitalistic tirade. Certainly the people living in East Germany in 1978 would have done anything to live in a world like this (my Gen-Z friends, if you don't know what I am referencing, please put this book down and read something about the communist world of the 20th century). Nevertheless, this consumption-based lifestyle has created some significant problems for humanity. Climate change, the obesity crisis, drug abuse, and chronic disease are just a few of the problems we can point to a society that has deemed its whole purpose as buying shit. However, these are all problems we understand as a society. If we eat the wrong food, it's bad for our health. If we consume the wrong energy, it's bad for the planet. Yet, when it comes to how consumption affects our brains, we have completely missed the mark.

What we are consuming matters to our mental health and overall well-being. This realization came to me in a classroom when I was sixteen. We have all had transformational teachers in our lives. One day, I mentioned to my geometry teacher Mr. Brennan that I was listening to an Odd Future song. He was a younger teacher and soccer coach, the kind of guy who got all of your references and wore cool sneakers to class. When I told him what I was listening to, he got stone faced and said to me, *"Garbage in, Garbage out Pat"*. Up until that very moment, my sixteen-year-old brain had never contemplated that the music I was listening to actually had any effect on me. Much like anyone else, I had formed my preferences in media on what I liked but also was cool enough that I wouldn't get made fun of for liking. At no point had I considered what value the music I was listening to actually provided.

Let's go back to that Odd Future song. Here are some of the lyrics from the song "Oldie" I was blaring on wired headphones attached to a school issued laptop:

> *"It's still Mr. Smoke-a-Lotta-Pot, get your baby mommy popped*
>
> *With my other snobby bop, do I love her? prolly not*
>
> *Know your shit is not as hot as anything I fuckin' drop*
>
> *Bitch, I'm in the zone, stand alone, like Macaulay Cock"*

Poetry really. (Don't take this as a knock on Hip-Hop, there are rappers with better use of iambic pentameter than Shakespeare). Now, I am sure you are much smarter than I was at sixteen. Your tastes have matured with time, and you have rounded your pallet. For me, one of the hardest truths I had to reconcile with during my mental health journey is that much of what I was consuming was stirring a lot of the problems in my life. In fact, my whole relationship to consumption was stirring up a lot of the unfulfilled feelings that lived inside me. This chapter, I will be asking you to do the same, to <u>reconcile with your consumption patterns</u>.

Orientation and Consumption

A lot of our problem with consumption is our relationship to the things we consume. We hear this all the time, specifically about food and drugs. While this is true, it should be expanded to all of our consumption patterns. There are a couple of consumption orientations that are specifically damning to our brains.

Pacifier Consumption: When you consume things just because it passes time, makes you feel momentarily good, or takes away from another emotion or stress of your current day.

- E.g. Fast Food, Reality TV, Drugs, Porn, News and TikTok

Confidence Consumption: Things we do or buy to 'flex' or prove our worth through purchases.

- E.g. Designer clothes, cars you can't afford, meals you only eat to make a TikTok, Instagram Vacation

Now, I am not trying to demonize every purchase you make. I assure you living in the woods would probably not be a better life (ok, maybe it would be). However, when we go into our consumption habits with the expectation to fill a void, you will be left with a shallow feeling. No purchase is fulfilling. However, once again by shifting our orientation to how we consume, we can find a more fulfilling and enriching way to spend our time and hard-earned dollars. We can do the same act but change our orientation to it, thus shifting our consumption orientation. For example:

Appreciation Consumption: Consuming something to appreciate the craftsmanship, artistic value, or positive feelings it may give us.

- **How?** E.g. Watching a movie to appreciate the great acting, eating a meal to enjoy the ingredients and chef, going on a vacation to enjoy a different culture, commenting on a TikTok because it made you happy.

Curiosity Consumption: Consuming because you want to experience something new or different.

- **How?** E.g. Watching a new TV show outside of your typical comfort zone, going to a bar in town you'd never normally go to, trying a new food.

Learning consumption: Consuming something to learn a new skill, expand your understanding of a subject matter, or improve on a skill/hobby/career you enjoy.

- **How?** E.g. Going to a cooking class, watching a YouTube video about your favorite musician, throwing on a documentary.

Generosity Consumption: Buying something as a gift, or as a way to make others' lives better.

- E.g. Buying a language software to better understand your partner's parents, getting a safer car to keep you kids out of harm's way, donating to charity

Consuming is a part of our life. How we approach our consumption can make a huge difference. We lose the opportunity to experience the most enriching parts of our lives by doing it mindlessly. When you go on that vacation, do it because you want to relax or learn something, not because your friends will be jealous of your post on social media. If you buy that designer handbag, only do it because you like it, or appreciate the craftsmanship, not because there is a Louis Vuitton sized hole in your heart. Buy the great car not because it will impress your friends, but buy it if you love the feeling of the summer wind hitting your hair with the windows down on a summer's afternoon. Some of the best meals of your life could be at a chain restaurant, it's just about how you think about it. None of your consumption needs to be fancy or expensive. Four hours away you can probably find a culture distinctly different from yours. There is a menu item at your local dinner they specialize in and are proud of that you can go appreciate. Finding the value in what we consume because of our appreciation for its value or the effort of those who made it is much more fulfilling than consuming to fill a hole inside us or show off to our friends. Most importantly, we need to orient ourselves to how we consume so we can find the things in our life that actually add value.

The Fear Economy:

Discussing what I am about to do without stepping on a political landmine will be difficult, so bear with me folks. Making you sad, scared, or mad is very profitable. News outlets, and social media providers know this all too well. Both know you are much more likely to engage with media that pisses you off or makes you scared more than anything actually valuable - in fact their entire profit model depends on it. Getting you addicted to the next news story that's going to infuriate you is just a mechanism to keep your eyeballs on the screen and keep you watching ads. A well thought out discussion from multiple different viewpoints with disagreements, counterpoints, and nuance is not possible in 140 characters on Twitter (I know it's X now, but I don't trust Elon not to change the name back before this book comes out) or on a news show before they have to cut to commercial. Matt Taibbi, whose claim to fame is the definitive analysis on the 2008 financial crisis for Rolling Stone

Magazine left traditional news media because he felt it was doing more harm for the average consumer than good. In his book *Hate Inc.: Why Today's Media Makes Us Despise One Another* he quotes an executive of a major news network who stated:

> *"In fact, the tension between the sheer quantity of horrifying news and your real-world impotence to do much about it is part of our consumer strategy.*
>
> *We create the illusion that being informed is a kind of action in itself. So to wash that guilt out—to eliminate the shame and discomfort you feel over doing nothing as the world goes mad— you'll keep tuning in."*

It's an easy, almost noble path to tumble down. Any good-hearted person wants to see the world as a better place. So when you are constantly fed information that says the contrary (in a constricted view), it leads you down a road of obsession. That obsession then gets tied deeply to your sense of self. Your ideas go well beyond just ideas and become a part of your identity. Now disagreements with your opinions aren't just differences in ideas, but you feel as if they are attacks on you as a person. Subsequently, you seek only information which validates those viewpoints, that information comes from sources who do that in a way that makes you mad or scares the shit out of you because at the end of the day - that's their business.

Social media has taken this a step forward. Now not only are you receiving a simulcast of the worst atrocities on Earth on your phone, like a keystone pipeline of human suffering, but the people providing it know literally everything about you. So not only are you getting upsetting content, you are getting content they know will specifically upset you. How fun! The chronicles of how social media has shifted our political landscape have been well documented. What's beneath an ever-growing polarization in our political sphere are behaviors that are making many unknowing people incredibly sick. The end state of a fully captured social media news consumer is either a.) becoming a complete extremist with no grasp of reality or b.) a person fully trapped by the paranoia of their fellow man. The social media companies know this to be true. Frances Haugen, a brave former Facebook employee (and co-creator of Hinge) came out in 2021 against her own employer as a whistleblower. She exposed that Facebook was not only well aware of the damage they were causing to their users and greater society, but they were doing nothing about it:

> *"Facebook Inc. knows, in acute detail, that its platforms are riddled with flaws that cause harm, often in ways only the company fully understands... Facebook makes more money when you consume more content. People enjoy engaging with things that elicit an emotional reaction and the more anger that they get exposed to, the more they interact and the more they consume."*

You are probably not to the level of a January 6th rioter, or a Just Stop Oil protester gluing themselves to the Mona Lisa (not calling these equivalent, just citing examples). Most of us are not in extremist cults or scared to go outside. That does not negate your news consumption is causing a mental health nightmare. From the scale of completely unaffected to fully captured, you more than likely reflect the latter more than you would like to admit. The human brain was not meant to diagnose all of the world's ills simultaneously. Our fearful responses were built for the limited context of the tribes we roamed with. On a typical day, an American teenager can be exposed to more atrocities on TikTok than an ancient Viking would see in their lifetime. Even 10 years ago, it was not uncommon for teenage boys to see an ISIS beheading video (those were all on YouTube and had more views than I'm comfortable sharing). For most of us, we don't take up arms or become activists, but we do grow an inherent fear of our neighbors. When the only current events you are receiving are the worst elements of humanity, you begin to become suspicious of any stranger you encounter. My boomer readers, have you ever wondered why young people don't just walk up to strangers and start a conversation? It's partially because we all have seen hundreds of true crime stories with seemingly normal people doing unspeakable things. However, when we zoom out, the world is a significantly safer place than it ever has been in human history. For instance:

About 70% of the world's population lived in extreme poverty in 1960, **today it's 10%**[17].

In 1950, 35% of the world's population could read, **now 85%**[18].

In the past century, the probability of fatalities in various scenarios has significantly decreased: the likelihood of death in a car crash has dropped by **96%**, pedestrian accidents by **88%**, plane crashes by **99%**, workplace fatalities by **95%**, and deaths from natural disasters including droughts, floods, wildfires, storms, volcanoes, landslides, earthquakes, or meteor strikes, by **89%**[19].

By all major statistics you are living in the physically easiest, safest, and most charitable time in human history. Yet, we are all paranoid of our neighbors. One of the most popular Christmas gifts purchased on Amazon yearly is a Ring doorbell. Suburban America feels so unsafe we are installing security cameras with live stream functionality to our front

---

[17] Desjardins, Jeff, and Niccolo Conte. "These 6 Eye-Popping Charts Show How the World is Improving." *Visual Capitalist*, 28 February 2018, https://www.visualcapitalist.com/6-charts-show-world-improving/. Accessed 13 February 2024.

[18] Desjardins, Jeff, and Niccolo Conte. "These 6 Eye-Popping Charts Show How the World is Improving." *Visual Capitalist*, 28 February 2018, https://www.visualcapitalist.com/6-charts-show-world-improving/. Accessed 13 February 2024.

[19] Pinker, Steven. "Steven Pinker: Is the world getting better or worse? A look at the numbers | TED Talk." *TED Talks*, 30 April 2018, https://www.ted.com/talks/steven_pinker_is_the_world_getting_better_or_worse_a_look_at_the_numbers/transcript. Accessed 13 February 2024.

doors. That fear does not match reality. This is not to say there are no crises that need to be solved, but our view of the world is misaligned with our current state. The constant access to the worst information possible about a very slim part of our population doing most of the heinous acts makes us all fear each other. That fear is completely avoidable only through reconciling our consumption of fear-based media.

First things first, you probably need to consume less news from all sources. I am not telling you to be uninformed or not to keep up with current events, but our citizenry was more informed (albeit, potentially misinformed) with a newspaper in the morning and an hour of news at night. Now you can't log onto Facebook without getting a full editorial on the southern border from your uncle Jim-Bob. Back to our initial problem, overstimulation, news, and current events are an incredibly easy way to get overstimulated. Most of the videos we see or stories we read are inherently shocking. Often this calls us to some action. However, really the only action we can normally take is to consume more. While yes, understanding a story in its totality is important, we often are not doing that. More likely you are finding opinions that reflect your own for personal gratification. Deepening your argument for a sense of being right, rather than for actually bettering the human condition. Also, we tend to find interest in anything that puts down ideas we don't agree with. This can be done tactfully and with respect, but those sources are few and far between. Purely in an effort to destimulate, walking away or taking stock in how much of the news or current events you're taking in should be a part of anyone's media diet. There is also something to be said on where you are getting your news from. Secondly, you need to ask yourself what value it's providing you, when we think about news or current event consumption, it normally falls into three consumption categories, **pacifier, curiosity, or learning consumption.** The most common and harmful way we consume news and current events is pacifier consumption, and it looks like this:

Pacifier Consumption: Watching, reading, or listening to current events that:

1.   Reinforce your current world view without appropriate or honest pushback.

     or

2.   Cause you anger toward your fellow man based on stereotypes or group typecasts (E.g., People from X political party have formed their opinion because they are stupid).

     or

3.   Mindless scrolling or watching with no intention other than the passage of time.

To change our consumption habits we must change how we orient ourselves to the news and events we are consuming. Let's look at some healthier ways to approach an information diet.

Curiosity Consumption: Consuming information in the effort to:

1.   Better understand our society

2.   Discover a world problem that we can take into account to better empathize with environments similar or dissimilar to our own.

Learning Consumption: Consuming information in the effort to:

1.   Make more informed voting or economic decisions.

2.   Information directly correlates to your career, school, or passion.

The vast ocean of news and information is scary. However, if we know what the goals are of the people giving us the news or information, we can better defend ourselves from its inadvertent effects. The news should be informative, not addictive or pacifying. Anything that leads us down a road of distrust for our fellow man (by the way, I am saying man in the royal sense, I don't mean just men) is not informative, it's personally destructive. When consuming news and events, use a critical eye. Separate your opinions from your identity, more than likely you are wrong about something, and that's ok! Growing in a lifetime means your ideas of how the world works should change. Each side of the political aisle has become more sensitive and isolated. The more we shelter ourselves from new viewpoints, the more likely we are to be missing opportunities to grow. Treating your aligned political doctrine like religion that can't be checked is not a healthy outlook, its fanaticism. Seek an outlook that constantly challenges your perspectives, while that may be difficult, is much less harmful to your psyche in the long term than a state of rage. Most importantly, constantly check your orientation. If the news isn't providing value to your life, or how you can impact the lives of others, walk away.

Food:

What you're putting in your mouth is a key factor in brain function. In order to truly transform into the mental state you desire, you will need to reconcile your eating habits. Now, this is not a weight loss conversation. Nor is it a conversation about body image. I dare not venture into those waters. Also I have nothing but empathy for how difficult those challenges are in a modern context. This is a much different conversation, one directly about how our behavior, mood, and mental wellbeing is being affected by the food we eat. Before you ask, no this isn't a *"the government is putting chemicals in the food to control your mind man"* conversation either.

Have you ever looked at a Hot Cheeto and thought *"you know, this color doesn't seem right"*? Now surely we all know pressed lumpy corn, flavored with hellfire and dyed a color meant to reflect Satan himself is good for us. No one cracks open a Mountain Dew Baja Blast with the idea that it's going to cure cancer. Nevertheless, have you ever considered what the firehose of chemical soup we pump into our bodies on a daily basis does to our brains? To get us started, here is a list of common chemicals in the American diet and their effects on our brains:

Nitrates: Increased risk of depression and bipolar disorder.

- Found in: Ultra Processed Meats

Red Dye 40: Banned in the U.K., Switzerland, Norway, Finland, France, and Austria[20]. ADD/ADHD, immune disorders, mind storms (misfires of the brain's wiring or electrical activity)[21].

- Found In: Sodas, candy, deserts, red snack foods.

BVO (brominated vegetable oil): Banned in Europe, Canada, and China[22]. Elevated levels of bromine have been linked to neurological manifestations such as memory impairment, tremors, fatigue, and headaches.

- Found In: Any citrus soft drink, "fruit flavors" processed fruit juice.

Sugar: Increased chance of mood disorders, higher levels of anxiety, weakened ability to respond to stress, higher risk of depression, impaired functions including decision making and memory and is highly addictive with massive withdrawal symptoms (anxiety, irritability, confusion, fatigue)[23].

- Found in: fucking everything.

---

[20] Sagon, Candy. "8 Foods We Eat That Other Countries Ban, Artificial Food Additives." *AARP Blogs*, 25 June 2013, https://blog.aarp.org/healthy-living/8-foods-we-eat-that-other-countries-ban. Accessed 20 February 2024.

[21] Amen Clinics. "What is Red Dye 40? ADHD And Brain Health | Amen Clinics Amen Clinics." *Amen Clinics*, 24 October 2023, https://www.amenclinics.com/blog/brain-health-guide-red-dye-40/. Accessed 20 February 2024.

[22] Sagon, Candy. "8 Foods We Eat That Other Countries Ban, Artificial Food Additives." *AARP Blogs*, 25 June 2013, https://blog.aarp.org/healthy-living/8-foods-we-eat-that-other-countries-ban. Accessed 20 February 2024.

[23] Marengo, Katherine. "Your Anxiety Loves Sugar. Eat These 3 Things Instead." *Healthline*, 23 June 2020, https://www.healthline.com/health/mental-health/how-sugar-harms-mental-health#withdrawal. Accessed 20 February 2024.

That's just to name a few of many that are causing serious harm to your mental state. Most of the chemicals flying in our mouths today were developed during World War 2. For those who fell asleep in high school history class, America during the war became the hub of essentially all goods created to equip and feed America and its Allies. Germany's bomb raids and land grabs across Europe left the U.S.A as the only viable economy to support the war. America fully industrialized, if you weren't fighting, you worked in a factory producing something for the war effort. Factories popped up like trees for the entirety of the war. Feeding a country while its economy is dedicated to stopping the Nazis is tough business. After the war, America returned to its peaceful state and needed to find a way to repurpose its many new factories now that tanks and guns had no buyers. Simultaneously, many innovations popped up to make quick and inexpensive food that could travel long distances. The American families strapped by the war effort, on the heels of the great depression needed cheap meals as much as the boys overseas (plus saving a few bucks goes a long way in war). These innovations are the foundations of what we now know as "processed" foods. Essentially everything you buy in a grocery store that's not a fruit, vegetable or meat can trace some roots this time period. With the boys back home, and America experiencing a new cultural revolution, these processed foods were all the rage. Who wouldn't love the idea of a 15-minute delicious dinner? Especially as women finally were making strides in the workforce. Fast forward three quarters of a century later and now you can buy something called a *Quesarito* that has what you can barely legally qualify as having meat inside (and it's delicious). The obesity crisis is the Nazis fault. Who knew! Add that to the fuck Hitler list. Never did our great grandparents consider that wartime crisis food is probably not good for us.

In the modern day we have to face a tough truth, most of our food is ultra processed garbage. In fact, 72% of the U.S. food supply is made up of ultra processed food[24]. We all know its garbage, but on average the ultra-processed version of a food is 52% cheaper than its holistic counterpart[25]. If you currently don't have the financial means to rid your body of abject toxic waste that's crushing your mental health, I understand. Growing up, Hot Dogs and Velveeta Shells and Cheese was a great occasion (delicious one at that). Our food system has made it virtually impossible to eat completely clean. Even more than cheap, ultra processed foods are addicting. The amount of sugar an American consumes daily is as addictive as heroin[26]. If Big-Mac trees grew in the wild our ancestors would be there every day, doesn't mean we were built for it. Truthfully, it's not strictly a monetary decision. The average meal at McDonalds rings in around $10, that's 1.5 dozen eggs. *"bUt pAT, eGGs arE HiGh in ChOlestErol"*. Yes, eating is really just a tradeoff. No one would argue you wouldn't be better off eating five eggs than a big mac. I am not asking you to be a superhero. Enjoy your food and your life, but understand that eating every meal of ultra processed food is extremely damaging to your mental health. There is no one size fits all solution. That said, there is a solution that works for you and your current finances.

Trading Up Choices: This is the simplest technique to enhance your food consumption for your mental health. When you go to eat, take the decision you were going to make, and move to the next best option. At the drive thru at McDonalds? Maybe get the meal, but sub in water. Planning a dinner for your family? Have the spaghetti dinner, but sub a side salad for the garlic bread. These little improvements over time will

---

[24] Stollman, Tamar, et al. "Database Indicates U.S. Food Supply Is 73 Percent Ultra-Processed – Food Tank." *Food Tank*, 30 November 2022, https://foodtank.com/news/2022/11/database-indicates-u-s-food-supply-is-73-percent-ultra-processed/. Accessed 21 February 2024.

[25] Stollman, Tamar, et al. "Database Indicates U.S. Food Supply Is 73 Percent Ultra-Processed – Food Tank." *Food Tank*, 30 November 2022, https://foodtank.com/news/2022/11/database-indicates-u-s-food-supply-is-73-percent-ultra-processed/. Accessed 21 February 2024.

[26] New York Post. "Why sugar, cheese and fast food are more addictive than heroin." *New York Post*, 27 February 2021, https://nypost.com/article/why-sugar-cheese-fast-food-are-so-addictive/. Accessed 21 February 2024.

do wonders for decreasing your chemical load and getting your mind back in a reconcilable place.

Does this fry smell like toxic waste?

I am beyond sorry for what I am about to do. Have you ever wondered why McDonald's fries are so good? There is no better feeling than digging your hand in the bag and stealing a few of those bad boys before you get home.

Well, as Michael Pollan pointed out in his brilliant talk *"You'll Never Eat McDonald's French Fries Again After Watching This"*, how those fries make their way to your mouth is grosser than Andy Dufresne's escape to freedom. If there is anything McDonalds demands its consistency. They want a quarter pounder to be exactly the same from Mumbai to Miami. Additionally, presentation is key, especially for the fries. That big flowering top of shiny golden potato goodness in a red box is like a symbol of American pride. This requires the potato to be long, and blemish free. For consistency of taste, all potatoes used to make the fries are Russet Burbank Potatoes grown on one farm in Idaho. These potatoes have the long part down, but almost always suffer from Net Necrosis. This causes spots to form on the potatoes. Because McDonalds will not buy a potato with a blemish, the farmers hose down their fields with a pesticide called Monitor. **This pesticide is so toxic farmers can't go out to their fields for 5 days after spraying at the risk of poisoning.** After harvested, the potatoes are taken to a warehouse sized shed that's atmospherically controlled to **let the chemicals breathe off for 6 weeks** before they are deemed ok for human consumption.

The Problem with Nostalgia

Oh the comfort of yesterday. We all yearn for simpler times. I was recently scrolling on twitter and there was a group of Gen-Alpha's yearning for the simplicity of 2020. I came to find out, this is not an aberration. I went down a rabbit hole and found slews of people talking about how much they missed gaming with their friends, chatting online, or time spent at home. Now there is something deeply disheartening the greatest memories of a child's formative years being spent around no actual humans. Now I don't know if you remember just four years ago, but I don't seem to remember being locked in my house, watching cities on fire, having the most contentious presidential election of our lifetimes and hearing a drunk uncles take on all of it on Facebook every day and thinking *"these are going to be the good old days"*. This may be an extreme case, but you have probably done something similar. Wished you were back in a different time in your life, a time that feels simpler with our modern view. Our media is full of people looking for a simpler time in our life. Every TV show is a reboot. Fuller House, Roseanne before she got really high on Ambien and tweeted a bunch of racist comments in the middle of the night, for god's sake they rebooted Fraser, WHO ASKED for a Fraser reboot? Every movie is based on our childhood icons (Barbie, Marvel, DC, Top Gun, Transformers, Star Wars, Live Action Disney remakes) and if we're lucky an occasional A24 film. Are we such emotional hemophiliacs we can't take the stress of a new story? We have become addicted to the nostalgia loop.

Looking through our old pictures, life looks so much easier. The truth is, it wasn't easier, you just know the ending of the story. You've left behind the troubles of that time because you passed them. You know the resolutions of the conflicts of the past, so no stress comes of them. This isn't always true, certainly moments tied to traumatic periods in our lives can have the opposite effect. It still remains true that as we pull further away from the events of a day, its worries fade, because we solved those problems. We look at pictures of our prom nights with glee at our skinny faces but don't remember being shuttled around all day with a beads of sweat rolling down our ass. Our constant need to relive our past is simply an avoidance technique of the present. We are dodging the challenges of today with a selective view of yesterday's feelings. Nostalgia most of all is a defense mechanism against uncertainty. Any human on Earth should have concerns about their future, and as you should. You have no idea what new challenges will greet you on the horizon. The past has certainty. You know Iron Man will beat the bad guy, you know Michael Scott will make the same joke he did the last twelve times you watched this Office episode, and you know when you look through your Facebook memories that you made it through that time. When we do this in a "looking at the good old days" way and not an introspective one it becomes our number one source for **pacifier consumption.**

Listen, I fucking love Harry Potter. There is nothing wrong with holding onto the things you love. Our life should be a compilation of all of our experiences, not just our most recent. It becomes damaging when we ruminate on a time we aren't currently in. It's easy to gain jealousy of your own past self. By avoiding today's feelings with yesterday's feelings it only serves to prevent us from enjoying the positive parts of today. Don't become the old man at the bar talking about how he could have won a state title, enjoy today.

Music, Movies, TV, Video Games

I feel like by this point you get the picture. For Music, Movies, TV, and Video Games I could go on another diatribe about how we are all wasting away. Let's just save it. Simply, evaluate if what you are watching or listening to is enriching your life. If it's not, change your orientation to it, watch something different or walk away.

Screen Time

Isn't that notification on your phone every Sunday about your screen time horrifying? It's like a push notification recap of all of your wasted time. A light buzz in your pants followed by a notice of your sin. We know we are on our phones too much, so why do we keep looking at them? My friends, I have some bad news. We are addicts.

We have covered how social media companies' sole purpose is to hack your ancient brain to keep you on the screen as long as possible. The truth is, no matter how many people tell us kids to put down our phones, we are not going to. You can't exist without that electric light box in your pocket. For all its faults, it's made the human experience significantly easier. By this point you are very aware I am going to tell you most of what you do on your phone is **pacifier consumption**. Here are a couple of really easy tricks you can do to be conscious of your phone consumption, and also limit it.

Dopamine Detox: Delete all of your social media apps for a day at a time. Like any drug, using it more is going to build a tolerance. It takes longer and longer to have that "How long have I been scrolling?" feeling. Start with 24 hours of deleting all your social media apps from your phone. I promise you will not realize how much you grab for your phone in a day. The next day you will be much more aware every time you go for TikTok instead of looking up. I suggest doing this on a day that you would typically use a lot of social media like a lazy Sunday or a travel day etc.

See how long you can go. I work a detox into my calendar every three months. For one week every three months I delete all the social media apps on my phone. Day one I feel like a junkie in withdrawal (even if you don't use your phone often, you'll be surprised how much "often" means in a modern context), but by day three you will have the mental clarity of Bradley Cooper in Limitless. When I redownload my apps after a week, I find I use them significantly less. Social media is a powerful tool, but addictive and a reset can get you in a healthy consumption zone. I suggest starting with one day, and building taking a week off into your routine.

Following Audit: When was the last time you looked through who you are following? If you are obsessive over how people will look at your follower ratio this applies to you especially. (For my older readers, people are extremely judgmental of who you follow versus who follows you.) Regardless, you should take stock in who you are following and what value they provide to you. If they are a pacifier, unfollow, and if they are providing content actually valuable to your life, keep them. Spending 15 minutes to go through who your following can dramatically change the value you're receiving from social media.

Algorithm Cleanup Crew: Social media companies, those little rascals have figured out how to show us what we want without even asking for it. TikTok, Twitter (X), and Instagram have gotten specifically good at this. The Instagram reel function, all of TikTok, and Twitter's "for you" functionality are all filled with content that is built perfectly for you. This is great in theory, but in practice we can't control what emotional response or consumption pattern will get us hooked. To combat this, we have to manually clean up our own algorithm. Every one of these apps has a *"I am not interested in this kind of content"* feature. Take the first 20 posts the algorithm feeds you and evaluate what kind of consumption that specific piece of content is. If it's something that is a pacifier, or evokes an emotion you don't like, mark the *"I am not interested in this kind of content"* button. Doing this once a month will manually scrub out the parts of our algorithm that are causing us harm, letting us use social media as a tool of value for our lives. Doing this at the end of a Dopamine Detox is a great way to approach our consumption habits with a fresh perspective.

The Vanderpump Rule

Listen man, life is hard. You can't always consume things that are enriching your life, sometimes you just want garbage. That's ok. In fact I encourage it. Dwayne "The Rock" Johnson has become famous for his wild cheat days. 6 days a week he is the model of human fitness, but once a week he goes crazy with a meal of his most craved food of the week. His "cheat days" are just as important as his discipline. The important part is he is setting the intention of what he's doing.

Our problems with overconsumption and constant stimulation stem from the mindlessness in which we do them. Consciously taking a moment for a splurge is perfectly ok. As long as we are orienting ourselves to it in a way that's honest, no harm is done. Binge watch the reality TV series, eat the whole can of pringles, play Call of Duty all day, just don't make it a consistency over the course of your week, and do so with the intention that it's your time to rest. You can't feel guilty over something you've planned to do.

Chapter 4:

The Brain and The Body

———— ❧❧ ————

"To keep the body in good health is a duty... otherwise we shall not be able to keep our mind strong and clear." ~ **Buddha**

Do you have hippie friends? You should. Sure, you'll hear endless nonsense about how crystals will recharge your energy and how Mercury in retrograde is a valid explanation for acting like a maniac, but a hippie will always bring some adventure to your life. That friend for me is a woman named Mariah, and she's the shit. On a warm spring day in Minneapolis where I was living at the time, she decided it would be a good day for an adventure. There is nothing quite like that first hit of Vitamin D hitting your skin after a brutal winter, suddenly every bit of sadness is washed from your body and being inside feels like a crime against humanity.

On this spring day, Mariah thought it would be a good idea to get our Tarot cards read. Such witchcraft would have horrified the southern Baptist church goers of my rural Virginia childhood, but the hit of sunlight dopamine made me believe this was a great idea. When we reached the location, we were shocked at the sight we saw. Despite a well-developed website, and good advertising the room, we walked into resembled an empty apartment with nothing but 4 chairs and two tables. They assured us the state of the building is because they were moving (I have checked in the years since, they haven't moved locations). The paint was peeling off of the walls, and the window unit AC was blowing lukewarm air into an 85-degree room, and the smell resembled death.

There was an old CD player style boombox playing chants. A man and a woman (presumably a mother and her son?) sat us on two of the chairs and closed the door behind them.

Immediately we were both terrified, I have seen enough horror movies to know this setup. Our new horrifying spiritual counselors let us know it would be $60 for them to read fifteen cards to us (it said $20 on the website), but if we gave them a 5 star review on Google BEFORE THE READING, the price would be $40. Now, if this were a normal scenario, we would have walked away, but with the clear possibility of being sold into human slavery as an option in this room, we gave the 5 stars and paid (on Venmo by the way, there was no cash register in this dungeon).

Mariah and I were then separated and taken on opposite sides of a literal shower curtain that was hung in this room separating the table settings to have our cards read. My cards were laid out in front of me by the woman who was incorrect in all of her assumptions about me, but I went along with the bit to see how far she could go. By the end of the conversation, the cards told me that my girlfriend (which I didn't have) was keeping me from exercising (which I do every day), and if I didn't start taking this woman's spiritual healing classes for $100 a week, I would die in a tragic skiing accident (I don't ski). Once we were done, the pair stood in front of the door hard selling us on services, Mariah looked at me and we burst through the pair and ran out of the building.

If there is any moral from that story (aside from bringing a knife with you to a psychic), it's that the internet has made lying incredibly easy. In doing the work and research to get my life back on track, I was met with 80% absolute nonsense. The nonsense was well presented and sold in a way that could fool most (including me, a lot). We all encounter this every day, whether it's your friend from high school selling for the newest pyramid scheme, or that guy on TikTok who only eats butter and claims it's the gateway to a healthy lifestyle. You are 3 clicks away from being fooled at all times. Nowhere more is that true than with our physical health. With that in mind, I want to be sensitive in writing this chapter. We all have been fed a lot of garbage information, specifically in how we take care of ourselves physically. It has made it almost impossible to discern the best steps to take in improving how we treat our body and its effect on our mental health. Also, the pressure on young women (and growing) on young men about body image makes this discussion incredibly more sensitive. Please don't take anything in this chapter to imply that your physical appearance is what's causing your mental health issues. I am not your doctor, and this is not a weight loss program. What we will be discussing is the direct correlation with how you treat your body and its effects on your brain. It's not just food and exercise, there are a multitude of factors about our physical state we need to take into account to become The Real Confident You.

Treating your body with kindness:

Self-love is an overused phrase in the modern lexicon. Millennials captioned their grainy 2013 ironic Instagram posts with it, and Gen-Z's creative take has been to call it a "self-love era" (the chokehold Taylor Swift has on our culture is insane, not a hater though, love Fearless). When it comes down to it, loving yourself is much harder than getting your favorite latte. Self-love is to treat yourself in a way that respects your own qualities and the value you bring to the world. How we treat our bodies is an expression of the respect we have for ourselves. If someone else treated you the way you treat yourself you would beat the shit out of them.

In our consumption conversation, we missed one key point, are you being kind to yourself? When you go to the gym, do you do it because you want to feel better, or are you punishing yourself? When you drink is it because you want to have fun, or is it because you can't stand the reality that you live sober? How we treat our bodies is how we view ourselves. Our actions are a display of our own self-respect. This is one of the hardest truths I have had to come to grips with. I have been a gym rat my whole life, but not because I wanted to feel better. It's because I was so insecure that any bit of extra weight meant I was a complete failure. Fucked up right? But I am sure you have felt similar feelings. When I started going to the gym with the <u>intention</u> of living a long life for my loved ones and having more energy, I got the life results I was looking for. As we go through a checklist of things you can do to improve your physical state to improve your mental state, keep in mind treating your body with kindness. Self-respect starts by you taking actions to respect yourself. Please do not beat yourself up if you aren't doing the things listed in this chapter, rather think about being kinder to yourself, and how to incorporate new ways to show yourself some respect.

Sleep

By all accounts, we are a sleep deprived society. ⅓ of Americans are sleep deprived[27], 50 to 70 million Americans have some type of sleep disorder[28], and 87% of high school students are getting less sleep than recommended. Whoever is selling Melatonin, buy that stock. Before you say, *"I can get 5 hours of sleep and be fine"*. People who don't actually need the recommended amount of sleep represents less than 5% of the population, so probably not you buddy. Sleep is essential to just about every piece of our mental health (and physical). Lack of sleep has been proven to cause poor stress coping ability, mood swings, poor appetite regulation, hormonal imbalance, increased anxiety, taxing effects on the cardiovascular system, temporary psychotic symptoms and even an

---

[27] Paprocki, Jonathan. "CDC: More than 1 in 3 Americans are sleep-deprived." *Sleep Education*, 28 September 2022, https://sleepeducation.org/cdc-americans-sleep-deprived/. Accessed 2 March 2024.

[28] Julia, Nina. "Sleep Statistics: Facts & Latest Data in America (2024 Update)." *CFAH.org*, 11 January 2024, https://cfah.org/sleep-statistics/. Accessed 2 March 2024.

increased risk of suicidal ideation[29]. Unfortunately, people with both anxiety and depression are both more likely to have sleep disturbances[30]. That said, the correlation could be linked to the behaviors of people with those disorders. Real chicken or the egg situation. Getting sleep is important for every facet of our lives. Yet, we put many blockers in our way to get quality sleep. Our phones, and general inability to destimulate has ruined our sleep patterns. Ever notice how great you feel on a Sunday morning? It's because you got 2 full nights of sleep.

Here is a good test to find out if you are getting quality sleep. Sleep deprivation is not just when you go to bed and when you get out, it's the quality of the sleep you are getting. From the time you close your eyes, it should take you no more than 15 minutes to fall asleep every night[31]. Also, you should only wake up once through the night[32]. Be honest, do you do both of those? If not, you need to address your sleep. Fear not insomniacs, here are some sure-fire ways to get to sleep quickly, and stay asleep.

---

[29] National Library of Medicine. "Short- and long-term health consequences of sleep disruption." *NCBI*, 19 May 2017, https://www.ncbi.nlm.nih.gov/pmc/articles/PMC5449130/. Accessed 2 March 2024.

[30] Cherry, Kendra. "How Does Lack of Sleep Affect Mental Health?" *Verywell Mind*, 23 January 2023, https://www.verywellmind.com/how-sleep-affects-mental-health-4783067. Accessed 2 March 2024.

[31] Sleep foundation. "How Long Should It Take to Fall Asleep?" *Sleep Foundation*, 19 December 2023, https://www.sleepfoundation.org/sleep-faqs/how-long-should-it-take-to-fall-asleep. Accessed 2 March 2024.

[32] Bahadur, Nina. "How Many Times Is It Normal to Wake Up at Night?" *Waking Up in the Middle of the Night: How Many Times Is Normal?*, 27 September 2018, https://www.self.com/story/nighttime-wakeups-frequency. Accessed 2 March 2024.

Bedtime for Bonzo: Checklist for Falling Asleep and Staying Asleep

1. *Put the phone away:* You need to destimulate to fall asleep. Beyond that, you need to remove as much light as you can before bed. Our brains set our internal clocks by our light exposure. 10,000 years ago, when the sun went down, there was no light, so you went to your cave and fell asleep. Our circadian rhythm (the system that regulates our sleep) when exposed to light, makes your brain think its daytime[33]. The flood of light coming from your phone or tv just before you sleep is telling your brain it's the middle of the day. To combat this, keep your phone away from your nightstand. If you use your phone as an alarm buy an alarm clock (they are like $12, if you can afford it get the kind that lights up your room in the morning). Try to get your lights as low as possible in the hours preceding bedtime, this will help alert your subconscious that it's night time.

2. *Box Breathe:* Counting sheep isn't perfect, but counting your breath helps. Tell me if you have been in this scenario before, your mind is racing in bed, and you can't fall asleep. You know you need to sleep, so now you are stressed out because you can't fall asleep, so you just think about trying to fall asleep. It's a vicious cycle we all fall into, and it happens because we are overstimulated. Some of our best thoughts come to us before bed (hell I thought of this book in bed) but getting to sleep is more important than late night thought chasing. If you can't get to sleep, start box breathing, but don't put an end to it. Focus on only your breath, and you will be asleep in minutes.

3. *Stop Eating Earlier:* Late night snacking is crushing your sleep quality. It takes several hours for our food to fully digest,

---

[33] Suni, Eric, and Dr. Abhinav Singh. "Light & Sleep: Effects on Sleep Quality." *Sleep Foundation*, 8 November 2023, https://www.sleepfoundation.org/bedroom-environment/light-and-sleep. Accessed 3 March 2024.

specifically moving food from your stomach to your small intestine which becomes much more difficult when you lie down[34]. Lying down with food in our stomach like this makes it surprisingly easy for stomach contents to back up into our throat while we are sleeping without us noticing (gross I know). Eating before bed gives us what is in essence heartburn the entire time we sleep. This can often explain morning breath (and why your morning breath is so nasty when you have been drinking alcohol all night and go right to bed). Also, consuming food triggers the release of insulin, which can interfere with your body's natural sleep-wake cycle by signaling wakefulness to the brain, thus making it harder to fall asleep[35]. Don't want to burn your throat all night? Stop eating two hours before bed as often as possible.

4. *Don't Chug Water Before Bed*: What's the most common reason we wake up in the middle of the night? It's because we have to pee. Anyone who bed wet as a kid knows you probably stop consuming liquid a couple hours before bed (where my bedwetters at?). That's often pretty hard, most people have a hard time hydrating throughout the day and night is the only time they can get their recommended daily values in. However, one specific habit causes a lot of unintended problems, chugging. When you chug a liquid, it makes your brain exacerbate urinary frequency and urgency[36]. When we chug, we pee. When we chug, we get up in the middle of the night to pee more often. We can probably link this to our

[34] Peters, Brandon. "Is It Bad to Eat Before Bed?" *Verywell Health*, 22 May 2023, https://www.verywellhealth.com/eating-before-bed-3014981. Accessed 3 March 2024.

[35] Cambridge University Press. ".,.", - *YouTube*, 6 January 2023, https://www.cambridge.org/core/journals/british-journal-of-nutrition/article/associations-between-bedtime-eating-or-drinking-sleep-duration-and-wake-after-sleep-onset-findings-from-the-american-time-use-survey/72A5D22C25A35FA975A5B50991431E0C. Accessed 3 March 2024.

[36] Clara. "Does chugging water make you pee?" *Hosh Yoga*, https://www.hoshyoga.org/does-chugging-water-make-you-pee/. Accessed 3 March 2024.

ancestors being much less likely to have consistent water on hand, so when they got to fresh water they drank A LOT, and our bodies developed a system to make space for all of this new water. So, in the couple hours before bed, and with that water on your night stand sip it as delicately as a princess, don't chug it.

5. *Your Bedroom is for Bedroom Things:* Try to keep as much stress out of your bedroom as possible. Doing work, or stressful things in your bedroom makes you much more likely to think about them as you are trying to doze off. Leave the laptop out of bed, and for the love of god don't answer an email in bed. Also, if you're arguing with your spouse, don't go to bed angry (that's a Kim and Al Broe tip, they met each other and after three weeks got married and have been together more than 30 years.)

6. *Stimulants:* Caffeine is a great drug for capitalism. I love coffee, but it can absolutely crush your sleep. The problem is how caffeine makes us alert. Caffeine keeps us alert by blocking adenosine, the brain chemical that puts us to sleep. When we are going to bed, caffeine is literally blocking our sleep process so no matter how tired you actually are, there is a chemical blocking the way. Don't drink coffee or any caffeine 8 hours before bed if possible. (and don't ever drink an energy drink, that stomach cancer in a can man)

7. *Magnesium Glycinate:* In terms of supplements you can take that will ensure a good night's rest, Magnesium Glycinate is safest and most effective. Many people will point you to melatonin, which in the short term is great. But due to the fact that it is a hormone our brain uses to sleep, building up a tolerance isn't probably a good idea (after a while you won't be able to sleep without it)[37].

[37] Bauer, Dr. Brent A. "Melatonin side effects: What are the risks?" *Mayo Clinic*, 2022, https://www.mayoclinic.org/healthy-lifestyle/adult-health/expert-answers/melatonin-side-effects/faq-20057874. Accessed 3 March 2024.

Additionally, there is a high chance if you are buying Melatonin, the product is tainted or deceptive. A study of thirty-one melatonin supplements found that concentrations could be anywhere from −83% to +478% of the dosage that was advertised on the bottle[38]. In fact, some Melatonin supplements have been found to be just CBD pills sold as Melatonin[39]. The U.K. and many other countries have banned selling it over the counter for this very reason. If you need Melatonin, get it from your doctor. Back to magnesium, given its relative abundance and needs of use beyond sleep you can be relatively assured that you are getting what you buy (like any supplement, please research the brand before purchase. The FDA does not regulate supplements and many of them are tainted.). Additionally, magnesium glycinate only helps regulate the neurotransmitters for our sleep chemicals, and it doesn't carry the dependance issues of melatonin[40]. If you are looking for a quick fix, magnesium glycinate will help. Please try the above first, supplements are meant to do that, supplement our behavior not replace it.

8. *Talk to a Doctor:* Last resort, talk to your doctor. Don't hesitate if you think you have a real problem. Sleep may be the most important part of your journey.

---

[38] National Library of Medicine. "Poor Quality Control of Over-the-Counter Melatonin: What They Say Is Often Not What You Get." *NCBI*, https://www.ncbi.nlm.nih.gov/pmc/articles/PMC5263069/. Accessed 3 March 2024.

[39] LaMotte, Sandee. "Potentially dangerous doses of melatonin and CBD found in gummies sold for sleep." *CNN*, 25 April 2023, https://www.cnn.com/2023/04/25/health/melatonin-gummies-wellness/index.html. Accessed 3 March 2024.

[40] Cleveland Clinic. "Does Magnesium Help You Sleep?" *Cleveland Clinic Health Essentials*, 28 June 2021, https://health.clevelandclinic.org/does-magnesium-help-you-sleep. Accessed 3 March 2024.

Sunlight and Vitamin D

In late 2022 a bearded extremely jacked man named "The Liver King" invaded most young men's algorithms. The Liver King promised that if you ate raw animal organs and lived life the way he did, you would be as jacked as he was. The Liver King had 3.6 million followers, or "primals" as he calls them, who were all convinced that raw beef liver was their ticket to salvation. Unsurprisingly it has since come out that Mr. Liver King is on an ungodly amount of steroids. This man's bathroom cabinet would have made Barry Bonds snitch. While this man's comical rise to fame and clear PED use has had him struck from most legitimate conversation, many of his followers found real change in their mental state because of the Liver King. No it wasn't the beef liver or sleeping on the floor (he really told people to do that), it was that he told his followers to get in the sun. Like most frauds, there has to be some grain of truth in what you are selling, and for the Liver King it was the sun.

Most people spend their entire day inside. The longest venture they have outside is the walk to a vehicle to take them to school or work. Our bodies were made to be outside. Until the industrial revolution nearly every human on Earth spent the majority of their day outside. Sunlight itself is a powerful tool our body is dependent on. Exposure to the sun produces chemicals that regulate our mood, our sleep cycle and has been proven to reduce both anxiety and depression symptoms for each additional hour spent in the sun[41]. The Liver King's followers weren't feeling happier because they ate testicles (really look this guy up, the protocol is hilarious), rather for the first time these young men's hormones were operating at normal levels because they got adequate amounts of sunlight. I know it's hard to get outside during the business of a day, but

---

[41] Wenk, Gary L. "Walking on Sunshine: The Light of Day Improves Mental Health." *Psychology Today*, 26 February 2022, https://www.psychologytoday.com/us/blog/your-brain-food/202202/walking-sunshine-the-light-day-improves-mental-health. Accessed 5 March 2024.

adding an extra 30 minutes of sunlight can make a world of difference for your life. This protocol is really simple, if you can be outside to do something, go outside. However, being that I have lived through a Minnesota winter, I understand sometimes it is literally impossible to get out. If that's the case, here is what I did.

1. No matter the weather, stand at your car door for 5 minutes before getting in it and look directly below the sun (not at the sun, I repeat not at the sun). The direct exposure to your face and through your eyes will give you the highest absorption potential. There is also data that suggests this kind of exercise in the morning and night will drastically improve not only your mood, but your sleep[42].

2. You can get some sunlight exposure through windows, open your shades during the day, and also try to get a desk at school or work that is close to a window.

Many of our benefits from sunlight are from Vitamin D. This chemical we get from the sun and some food is a miracle worker that reduces our risk of mortality, helps with weight management, reduces inflammation, and most of all regulates our mood/reduces depressive symptoms (it even keeps bones strong which is why some milk has it added)[43]. Our lack of sunlight can be attributed to many health problems and most importantly in this context is partially to blame for our mental health crisis. 42% of American adults and up to 70% of children under age 11 are deficient in Vitamin D[44]. Even with our best efforts to get in the sun,

---

[42] Huberman, Andrew. "Using Light for Health." *Huberman Lab*, 24 January 2023, https://www.hubermanlab.com/newsletter/using-light-for-health. Accessed 5 March 2024.

[43] Mayo Clinic. "Vitamin D." *Mayo Clinic*, 2024, https://www.mayoclinic.org/drugs-supplements-vitamin-d/art-20363792. Accessed 5 March 2024.

[44] National Library of Medicine. "Vitamin D Deficiency - StatPearls." *NCBI*, 17 July 2023, https://www.ncbi.nlm.nih.gov/books/NBK532266/. Accessed 5 March 2024.

our bodies need a certain amount of Vitamin D to come from our food. Here lies another modern issue, our food is less nutritious than it was 100 years ago. I am not talking about the difference between an orange and a cheeseburger. The fruit, vegetables and meat all contain less nutrients than they used to. Because of industrial farming, the world's soil has been stripped of all its nutrients. The University of Texas showed forty-three vegetables and fruits to have "reliable declines" in key nutrients[45]. The food we used to rely on for our Vitamin D frankly doesn't have it any more. So this leads me to the only time in this book I am going to tell you to take a pill. Go to your local drugstore and get a Vitamin D supplement.

Winter and Seasonal depression

Anyone who has lived in the most northern states of America will tell you seasonal depression is widespread. The areas of the country that experience extremely low sunlight in the winter months (upper midwest, pacific northwest, and northeast) experience significant spikes in depression during winter[46] (National Library of Medicine). In fact, my own suicide attempt happened in late January.

If you are in one of our frozen tundra states and experience depressive tendencies, please use some extra caution. Those months of gray days that seem exponentially longer trapped in your home feel like a state of purgatory you will never leave. Please, regardless of the weather, bundle up and get some sunlight on those cheeks and take Vitamin D. Plus we all know it's the wind, not the cold that will get cha'.

---

[45] Scientific American. "Dirt Poor: Have Fruits and Vegetables Become Less Nutritious?" *Scientific American*, 27 April 2011, https://www.scientificamerican.com/article/soil-depletion-and-nutrition-loss/. Accessed 5 March 2024.

[46] National Library of Medicine. "Seasonal Depressive Disorder - StatPearls." *NCBI*, 2023, https://www.ncbi.nlm.nih.gov/books/NBK568745/. Accessed 6 March 2024.

Drugs and Alcohol

Listen, I'm not a teetotaler. I drank like a fish in college, I smoked weed until I got so paranoid about the universe being mostly empty space I forgot to breathe, and more. Exploring substances is part of life. It helps us relax, find new meaning in our friendships, and get the courage to walk up to that person we may spend the rest of our life with. Modern humans with our general consumption problem, however, have a tendency to abuse these substances. Also we generally don't understand how they work. I debated heavily keeping this part of the chapter in at the chance of being preachy. This is not Nancy Reagan's "just say no campaign". The most important thing you need to address about your use of drugs and alcohol is your intention when consuming. Drinking to numb yourself? Probably stop. An occasional cocktail to celebrate a hard week of work with your friends? Not a big deal. As you evaluate if you are treating your body with kindness, take an evaluation of your consumption of substances and what your intention is when using them. Ok now it's time for me to go one by one and scare the shit out of you.

Alcohol

Alcohol has been normalized to a point in our society that we rarely weigh the physical consequences. Sure, we think about the hangover coming the next day, or maybe we know we will regret the dumb things we say but almost never do we weigh the physical consequences it has on us. I hate to be the bearer of bad news, alcohol is terrible for your mental health. Alcohol is a depressant, meaning its chemical effects slow down the central nervous system. This is why when you drink some of your functions are seemingly turned off, like fear. You danced on that table in college due to your subdued senses. The rational part of your brain is slowly turned off with each tequila shot until you're making out in the middle of the dancefloor with a stranger. That depressant effect, however, outlasts your drunken night. Alcohol leaves lingering effects of[47]:

1. Poor sleep, affecting mood and energy levels.

2. Worsening symptoms of depression and anxiety.

3. Causing memory loss and cognitive impairment.

For depressed and anxious people, alcohol is maybe one of the more sinister drugs to take. If you drink, your poor feelings seem to wash away. For a brief period you feel like you have a moment of escape from your depressed state. That part is great; what nefarious is when you are once again sober you are often much more depressed than when the bottle first hit your lips. So you enter a cycle, building your entire week up to the only moment of happiness on the weekends because you can finally feel numb. I fell into this. After college I entered the workforce and took an extremely stressful job at an even more competitive firm. The 80-hour work weeks were driving me insane, so the only thing I had to look forward to was a weekend numbness. It was only when the physical effects (I was getting fat) took over that I realized I needed to change something. Years later I look back with some fond memories, but mostly the realization that many people were doing the same thing. Want to know who your real friends are? Stop drinking. If you don't hang out with a person without drinking you don't have a friend you have a drinking buddy.

Let's be mindful about this, unless you have a substance abuse issue (which I am woefully under qualified to diagnose you with) there is no reason to stop drinking forever. There are moments in our lives when alcohol can be a great thing. Who would sit through the best man's

---

[47] Bhandari, Smitha. "How Does Alcohol Affect Your Mental Health?" *WebMD*, 15 May 2023, https://www.webmd.com/mental-health/addiction/what-to-know-about-alcohol-and-mental-health. Accessed 9 March 2024.

speech at a wedding without a few cocktails in them? Reconciling your alcohol use, however, can help you make great strides in finding <u>The Real Confident You</u>. Here are a couple sure fire ways to make sure your whiskey nights are a benefit and not a detriment to your life:

- **Sober October/Dry January:** Like with any substance or habit you aren't physically dependent on, setting some time away from it can be a great way to reset. You'll realize over the course of that month when you grab a drink and if it actually is necessary. There are a lot of sneaky drinks we don't think about (especially in our twenties). Taking one month off is a great time period to establish a healthy relationship with our drinking and also feel the mental health benefits of a depressant free lifestyle.

- **Go out without:** Ever wondered what that night out at the bar would look like to your sober mind? Try it. Don't tell anyone you aren't drinking, and do an activity you would typically drink doing. Order drinks that resemble booze (club soda with lime, red bull, etc.) and watch. I promise you'll be horrified enough to rethink next weekend's plan.

- **Limit the "sneaky drinks":** Is that *dollarita* with your Applebee's really doing it for you? Did you really need to get a gin and tonic at the after work happy hour? Do you need a glass of wine watching the bachelor on Tuesday (I would understand if this answer was yes)? Cutting out alcohol at times when we really don't need or want it but it's become reflexive to drink is a great way to reduce the chemical load. Every little bit helps in getting your mood back on track.

Meth, Cocaine, Prescription Drugs, Heroin, etc.

Remember our "everything in moderation, all that matters is your intention" convo? Does not apply here. Shouldn't have to tell you that.

Coffee is for Closers:

Yes, caffeine is a drug. A drug I couldn't have written this book without, but a drug, nonetheless. Caffeine is ubiquitous in modernity. It's impossible to find an American home without a coffee pot in it. 94% of American adults consume caffeine, 64% consume caffeine daily, and 56% consume the daily amount of caffeine equivalent to four or more cups of coffee[48]. Caffeine is a great tool. It helps us focus and achieve our goals. Hell, what would *Friends* be like if Ross and Rachel couldn't hang out in the Central Perk Cafe! Sounding like a broken record, an excess of caffeine can have some devastating consequences. Juxtaposed to alcohol, caffeine is a stimulant. It gets us perked up and ready to attack our day. Previously mentioned, caffeine blocks adenosine, one of our sleep-inducing brain chemicals. Additionally, it increases our heart rate and stimulates our central nervous system to make us alert[49]. Also it stimulates your digestive system (but you know this already I'm sure). This stimulation is great for focus, but also it stimulates our anxieties. That same drive that pushes you to get your work done also fosters much unnecessary anxiety. Having too much caffeine with our already persistent overstimulation problem is like pouring gasoline into a fire. The worst part about caffeine consumption is it sneaks up on us. Caffeine tolerances build relatively quickly, that morning cup of coffee first made us alert and now feels like a necessity just to feel like ourselves. Here are a couple easy ways to keep your caffeine in check:

---

[48] Peckham, Tina Smithers, et al. "94% of us Drink Caffeinated Beverages." *Sleep Foundation*, 26 September 2023, https://www.sleepfoundation.org/sleep-news/94-percent-of-us-drink-caffeinated-beverages. Accessed 9 March 2024.

[49] Olsen, Natalie, and Ann Pietrangelo. "The Effects of Caffeine on Your Body." *Healthline*, 7 August 2017, https://www.healthline.com/health/caffeine-effects-on-body. Accessed 9 March 2024.

- ***How does that make you feel?:*** Have you ever really taken stock on how your caffeine intake actually makes you feel? Sure you did when you first started drinking coffee, but now you just put it down the hatch and start your day. Drink your morning joe, set a timer for 30 minutes, and take stock in how you feel. If you don't like the feeling, it's probably time to make that double espresso a single.

- **Wait until later:** You're gonna hate me for this one, but having coffee first thing in the morning is not only terrible for your sleep, but it's making your caffeine intake less effective. Upon waking, even if you're groggy, your adenosine levels are typically at their lowest. It's advisable to wait 1.5 to 2 hours to let your body naturally awaken, aided by hydration, sunlight exposure, and gentle movement to stimulate morning cortisol production, and allow adenosine to accumulate slightly. By doing so, your first cup of coffee will not only offer a more pronounced sense of alertness (thanks to the buildup of adenosine), but it may also support the reinforcement of your natural sleep-wake rhythm. Delaying caffeine intake until later in the morning can reduce the likelihood of experiencing an energy slump around midday, thus aiding in avoiding caffeine consumption too close to bedtime[50].

- ***Read the Label:*** The recommended daily value of caffeine is below 4 cups of coffee or 400 milligrams[51]. That seems completely reasonable right? However, when you take into account that a cup means 8 ounces we run into issues. When you realize a Grande

---

[50] Huberman, Andrew. "Using Caffeine to Optimize Mental & Physical Performance." *Huberman Lab*, 4 December 2022, https://www.hubermanlab.com/episode/using-caffeine-to-optimize-mental-and-physical-performance. Accessed 9 March 2024.

[51] Mayo Clinic. "Caffeine: How much is too much?" *Mayo Clinic*, https://www.mayoclinic.org/healthy-lifestyle/nutrition-and-healthy-eating/in-depth/caffeine/art-20045678. Accessed 9 March 2024.

cup of coffee from Starbucks is 16 ounces, or that a typical latte is a ¼ of your daily value we run into problems. Sure you may only have 4 "cups" of coffee in a day, but when the cup itself you put it in is 12 oz's, we have a problem. Also, caffeine is hidden in much of our daily consumption. Take a Diet Coke, which has 46 mg in a can. Seems fine right? Well if you get the typical restaurant size it's more like 108 mgs, that's more than a 1/4th of your daily value. Moral of the story, track the amount of caffeine you are actually consuming and read your labels, so it doesn't run away from you.

Sourdough and Soaring Blood Pressure

When I go to Panera Bread, I am expecting a mediocre bowl of soup and an average baguette to pair with it. What I am not expecting is a lemonade that could kill me. In late 2023, Panera Bread came under fire for its "Charged Lemonade". The advertising did not make it apparent that there was caffeine inside of it. You could maybe infer from its name that it has some caffeine, but in its regular size it had **260 Mgs of caffeine**[52]. That's two Monster Energy drinks.

Due to the lack of an apparent caffeine warning, multiple people went into cardiac arrest after its release after consuming multiple and thinking it was a routine lemonade[53]. Clearly they are getting their pants sued off over this. Please, read the nutrition label, because Panera Bread has to be the worst cause of death imaginable.

---

[52] Powell, Carilee, and Jennifer Borrenson. "Panera's charged lemonade: See how it compares in caffeine content." *USA Today*, 12 December 2023, https://www.usatoday.com/story/graphics/2023/12/12/panera-charged-lemonade-caffeine-deaths/71851706007/. Accessed 9 March 2024.

[53] Zibler, Ariel. "Panera Bread moves its 'Charged Lemonade' behind counter after lawsuits over consumer deaths." *MSN*, 9 November 2017, https://www.msn.com/en-us/money/companies/panera-bread-moves-its-charged-lemonade-behind-counter-after-lawsuits-over-consumer-deaths/ar-BB1h5BKW. Accessed 9 March 2024.

Nicotine:

Remember around page 3 when I said I'm not your guru and still have plenty of problems of my own I am working on? This is one of those problems. I am a daily nicotine user. Being that anything I say would be hypocritical I'll refrain from my typical structure of over explanation followed by proverbial life hacks. Here is what I can say: nicotine is a stimulant, and all of the mental effects I listed for caffeine remain but the addictive nature is much higher. Any form of nicotine is not a great habit, and you should work toward kicking it. Here's to the chapter in my next book where I can tell you how to quit.

Weed:

Cheech and Chong seem pretty happy to me. The devil's lettuce is growing into its acceptance era in America. Despite Nixon and William Randolph Hearst's best efforts to keep the chronic out of the good people's hands, America is ready for its legal weed. 9/10 Americans are pro-Mary Jane legalization (and we can't agree on anything)[54]. As states continue to make ganga legal, it's fair to say we all need to take stock in our partaking of the herb. For starters, puffing that zaza is a viable form of medicine in many instances. For those experiencing pain, epilepsy, anxiety, and many other ailments there is serious medical backing showing potential benefits. However we all know people who smoke the sticky icky until 3 in the morning watching *Game of Thrones* for their "headaches". In the jazz grass's revolution, most potheads will tell you there are no downsides. However, this isn't Bob Marley's bud. Plant breeding has made dope much more potent than what Pink Floyd was

---

[54] Schaeffer, Katherine. "7 facts about Americans and marijuana." *Pew Research Center*, 13 April 2023, https://www.pewresearch.org/short-reads/2023/04/13/facts-about-marijuana/. Accessed 9 March 2024.

pulling from the bong. Depression, diminished libido, lower drive, and more can be associated with excess use[55]. Also, if you have schizophrenia in your family I would highly advise against it as weed can be a catalyst to dormant genes and give you full blown schizophrenia[56]. For the rest of us going back to our consumption patterns, why are you rolling a five finger blunt every night? If it's to be comfortably numb, it's not helping your life. I'll never tell you not to smoke (in fact I will tell you TO smoke and listen to Dark Side of the Moon while watching The Wizard of Oz with the sound off. Google it.) just make sure you're doing so in moderation and in a way that actually benefits your life.

Eat Half The Brownie

For my younger audience, you already know this. For my older audience who have all simultaneously discovered THC gummies in the last 5 years, this is for you. Eating weed and smoking weed are two very different things. When you smoke it is absorbed through your lungs as THC which is what makes you high. When you eat it, it's processed by your liver and gets turned into 11-hydroxy-THC which is 5x more psychoactive[57]. Layman's terms, you get way higher. However, because it travels through your digestive system this process is much slower. So please take your time. Despite what the packaging

---

[55] Schaeffer, Katherine. "7 facts about Americans and marijuana." *Pew Research Center*, 13 April 2023, https://www.pewresearch.org/short-reads/2023/04/13/facts-about-marijuana/. Accessed 9 March 2024.

[56] Schaeffer, Katherine. "7 facts about Americans and marijuana." *Pew Research Center*, 13 April 2023, https://www.pewresearch.org/short-reads/2023/04/13/facts-about-marijuana/. Accessed 9 March 2024.

[57] Leafwell. "What is 11-hydroxy-THC?" *YouTube: Home*, 9 November 2017, https://www.bing.com/ck/a?!&&p=e2937d3cd6e06d2dJmltdHM9MTcwOTk0MjQwMCZpZ3VpZD0xMzQ1ZmFmOS00MGIxLTZlYmEtMjdhNi11OGE0NDExOTZmMmUmaW5zaWQ9NTI2MA&ptn=3&ver=2&hsh=3&fclid=1345faf9-40b1-6eba-27a6-e8a441196f2e&psq=11+hydroxy+metabolite&u=a1aHR0cHM6Ly9sZWFmd2VsbC5jb5. Accessed 9 March 2024.

says the dosages are not regulated. 5mgs does not mean 5mgs. Every brand, dispensary and smoke shop will have varying effects for what is said to be the same dose. Because getting too high can turn you coo-coo for cocoa puffs, eat half the gummy bear and wait 30 minutes.

Exercise:

In my journey, no facet of life improvement has been more beneficial to me than exercise. We will talk later about how developing a skill will be essential to finding The Real Confident You, and for me I can say exercise has saved my life. I also am aware that it makes me one of the most annoying people on earth. Justifiably so, for many the gym isn't a very welcoming place. It's tied to memories of childhood and current insecurities. Walk into any gym in America and you are in some sort of sweaty jungle of half-naked people staring into mirrors and grunting. Also, it's not easy to do. Taking time out of your day to do something both physically and emotionally uncomfortable is a seemingly insurmountable task for most, and with gym goers apparent air of elitism most people's potential sense of achievement is robbed by judgmental stares of insecurity inducing onlookers. None of that changes the fact that a sedentary lifestyle is a large catalyst for many mental health problems.

I feel the need again to mention this is not a body image conversation. Physical fitness exists for many different body types, and your weight as it relates to your health is a conversation for your doctor not an Instagram influencer. For your mental health though, there is no more powerful tool in your belt than exercise. The statistics backing this up are staggering:

- Exercising for just 15 minutes a day reduces your risk of depression by 26%[58].

- Exercise encourages various transformations within the brain, such as the expansion of neural networks, decreased inflammation, and the development of new activity patterns that foster sensations of tranquility and overall wellness[59].

- Due to the growth of new neurons, exercise drastically reduces your body's reaction to anxiety[60].

- In a study done by the CDC of 1.2 million adults, compared to those that did not, participants who exercised regularly had 40% less bad mental health days then their non-exercising peers[61].

I have hundreds of these, would you like me to continue? The point is exercise is a lifesaving tool. If we think back to our ancestors, it makes perfect sense why our brain rewards being physically active. Movement meant we were doing something for ourselves or our tribe to be better off. Here is where the conundrum lies, as much as our body rewards us for effort it also likes comfort. Later we will dive deeper into this topic, but for now what you need to know is comfort is the default position of our bodies. That does not mean it's beneficial, in fact it's often detrimental.

---

[58] Help Guide. "The Mental Health Benefits of Exercise." *HelpGuide.org*, 5 February 2024, https://www.helpguide.org/articles/healthy-living/the-mental-health-benefits-of-exercise.htm. Accessed 10 March 2024.

[59] Help Guide. "The Mental Health Benefits of Exercise." *HelpGuide.org*, 5 February 2024, https://www.helpguide.org/articles/healthy-living/the-mental-health-benefits-of-exercise.htm. Accessed 10 March 2024.

[60] Gans, MD, Stephan. "The Mental Health Benefits of Physical Exercise." *Verywell Mind*, 3 January 2023, https://www.verywellmind.com/mental-health-benefits-of-exercise-2584094. Accessed 10 March 2024.

[61] UCLA Health. "The Link Between Exercise and Mental Health." *UCLA Health*, 17 October 2018, https://www.uclahealth.org/news/the-link-between-exercise-and-mental-health. Accessed 10 March 2024.

So how do you get active? I wish there was a silver bullet. I am one of those work out first thing in the morning workout weirdos. As Deion Sanders once put it *"I work out first thing because I get to set my own thermostat, I don't have bad days because they start the way I planned them every single time"*. Hard to argue with Coach Prime. But I certainly did not start this way. The biggest problem most have with exercise is biting off more than you can chew. It's January 1st, and you tell yourself *"this is the year"*. You throw out all the junk food in the fridge, buy a $300 gym membership, and buy a new pair of shoes. Walking into a gym overcrowded with resolutioners you work out with a shell of a program you used in high school with no goal but to "get in shape" or "lose 15 lbs.". Two weeks later you are eating the monthly fee of a gym you'll never go to again and the lettuce is getting wilted in your fridge. We set ourselves up for failure when we don't do the proper planning and intention setting. Remember the "University of Bath" study from earlier? Quick refresh, if you go to the gym aimlessly there is a 35% chance you'll stay consistent for the month, if you set clear goals not just for your end state, but what you will be doing every day there is a 91% chance you'll make it through the month. I'd take that bet. So how does one create a plan that you can actually stick to for exercise? Try this:

- ***Implementation Calendar:*** You have to take this thing one step at a time. Going into a gym thinking you can work out as hard as a Navy Seal on your first day is fucking insane. You have to start somewhere. This is a journey not a race, the important part is getting a little better every day. Plan your exercise into bite size pieces. Starting small is the best and only way to ensure you'll keep coming back. Here is an example of a calendar to follow:

Exercise Implementation

	Month 1				Month 2			
	Week 1	Week 2	Week 3	Week 4	Week 1	Week 2	Week 3	Week 4
Walk 3 Days a week	●							
Walk 5 days a week			●————————————————●					
Lift weights twice a week					●———————————————————————————————●			
Attend 1 fitness class a week							●————————●	

By starting slow and building you can ensure you have a plan that will simultaneously not overwhelm you and give you the improvement needed for mental health improvement.

- *Accountabilibuddies*: You don't have to be alone in this. Getting in an exercise routine is hard and finding someone to share that struggle with is helpful. I have a group chat called "The Brogrum" each morning the first thing we do is text the group chat "good morning" to let each other know you have gotten to the gym. We also use it as a space to encourage each other, ask questions, and be honest about what we are struggling with in the gym. It was said no better than Brogrum member Jack when he said, "For motivation I use the mental fear of disappointing the boys". Get a friend, and do it together.

- *Set Goals:* In future chapters we will discuss how not to set frivolous goals but giving it to you simply: a goal without a plan is a wish. Starting at an end goal of "what does good look like for me?" and building your plan backwards from there is the best way to have a plan, and goal that comes true.

However, that goal cannot be frivolous, meaning saying "I want to lose 15 pounds" is not a goal, at best it's a wish. You need to make sure your goal is clear, trackable, and achievable. Following the SMART framework you can make a goal that is just that. SMART goals are specific, measurable, achievable, relevant, and time-bound objectives designed to provide clear direction and increase the likelihood of success. By setting SMART goals, individuals can effectively outline their intentions, track progress, and attain desired outcomes within a defined timeframe. A smart goal in this context looks like "Over the next three months, I will engage in aerobic exercise for at least 30 minutes, five days a week, aiming to achieve a total of 150 minutes per week". This goal is specific, measurable, achievable, relevant, and time-bound, allowing you to improve your mental health and overall fitness by consistently incorporating exercise into your routine.

- *Follow a Program:* Let's be honest, you don't know that much about working out. I've worked out every day for a decade and am still constantly learning little improvements (also I still only look like an overfed 8th grader). Don't let your ego get in the way of improving your life. Men have a big tendency to do this, they worked out for high school sports and now think they could be a certified personal trainer. Go online and find a program that aligns with your goals and follow it. Having the planning done for you by someone who actually knows what they are doing will keep you accountable to your goals and make sure your efforts are successful. If you have the money, hire a good trainer.

- *Have Fun:* The most important thing about exercise is that somewhere along the way we forgot how fun it could be. Remember playing tag with your friends? If you do exercise right it's like that. Listen to your favorite music, or a book that makes you happy. Go on a hike, take a dance class, play basketball or anything that you actually have fun doing. The most important thing is to move, not where you do it.

Step 1: Complete

Congrats on completing step one! Look at you, reading a book and improving yourself. Take a bow! In the first part of this book we addressed your inputs. The direct or indirect patterns of consumption and environment that lead us modern humans down a road of unhappiness and mental illness. What we have addressed so far is true no matter where you currently are. Think of this as a foundation. When we are physically sick, we often first wonder what made us sick, and that is what the first part of this book laid out. So, whenever you are wondering why you may be heading down a road of unwellness, come back to this foundation. These things are always completely in your control and can take you back to a baseline that is ready to address larger issues. If a smoker goes into a doctor's office wondering why they are coughing, the doctor will tell them it's the cigarettes. The inputs you have just read about are your cigarettes, and even when a smoker quits it does not mean they are healed. In fact, it just means they have stopped doing more damage. When my friend Austin rolled his ankle playing volleyball, we wrapped it and elevated it. Fixing your inputs is like wrapping and elevation, it just gives you the opportunity to heal.

This next section of the book is for just that, healing the damage. Your mind is now at a state that can be remodeled. You didn't think finding real confidence would be as easy as watching less news and taking some vitamin D did you? This part may be uncomfortable. That discomfort is worth it on the path to being The Real Confident You, trust me. I've titled the next section "Doing the Work" because that's what it is, work. Finding The Real Confident You is a difficult but rewarding journey. My challenge to you in reading the next section is this, what part of your current state is your fault and what part isn't? Yes, as I have explained our environment has made it incredibly difficult to be a mentally healthy person. But you knew that already didn't you? Was anything I said in the first part of this book groundbreaking? I doubt you had a moment where your eyes were opened to a shockingly new reality. Everything you have needed to get better has been at your fingertips the entire time. Finding The Real Confident You means understanding your faults just as much as your positive attributes. You have many of both, what this journey should do is let you learn the realistic measure. Self-esteem comes from the self, finding it is a journey of which I can only take you to the road.

It's your adventure to travel and find. You'll fall and bump your knee more times than you can count. The important part is your doing it on a road leading to where and who you want to be and learning with every fall. You are not the one at fault for your current state, but you are the only one who can change it.

Oh, and have you been practicing your box breathing?

Part 2:
Doing The Work

Chapter 5:

The Self-Image dilemma

"No man, for any considerable period, can wear one face to himself and another to the multitude, without finally getting bewildered as to which may be the true." ~ **Nathaniel Hawthorne, The Scarlet Letter**

Everyone is a brand now. We all have a public persona and a private persona. Social media has commodified the human experience. Living for what our phones will tell the world about us is not only the norm, but the expectation. We don't take into account that watching the highlights of our friends' lives isn't their actual reality. No one's Facebook is indicative of their actual life. No, Abby doesn't only go to wineries with her gal pals and take idyllic pictures with her family. More than likely she was screaming at her kids before that smiling shot was taken and she spent the whole winery day complaining that her friend Bailee stole the spotlight at her wedding. But that's not the reality you see, rather you see smiling photos of Abby having the best day of her life. Without providing real thought to a check in of our network we can easily be bombarded with lives that look much more glamorous and happier than our own. Tack onto that the constant filtering and photoshopping we do to our photos, and not only do these photos not represent the actual life of a person, but they show a physical appearance widely better than reality. Human beings are designed to constantly evaluate where we are in a society. For our hunter-gatherer ancestors this made sense, after all a constant evaluation of how well you are doing in the tribe meant you would contribute more and the tribe would live on. The humans that contributed the most and were valuable probably stayed alive in the hardest of times and passed the coinciding social paranoia to us. This phenomenon is detailed eloquently by Will Stoor in his book *"The Status Game"* which he states:

> *"Researchers find our reward systems are activated most when we achieve relative rather than absolute rewards; we're designed to feel best not when we get more, but when we get more than those around us."*

In less academic language, we do not evaluate ourselves based on how well we are doing, but how well we are doing based on those around us. While it is probably unhealthy to focus too much on our status, there is unfortunately no hiding from the fact that our subconscious will always be keeping score. Back to social media, our evaluation of our own status is very skewed when we only see the best parts (and often over exaggerated) of others' lives. It's like competing in a sport where everyone else is on steroids. It makes us feel inadequate because we are unable to properly diagnose our own self-worth. Also, this causes us to lie to ourselves. The image we project is not that of who we are in reality. Glossifying our own lives creates a character we are never able to live up to. The superhero versions of us that live online don't reflect who we are in real life but make us think less of ourselves in comparison to a manufactured us.

Our self-image dilemma doesn't start and stop with social media. In the 1970s a new movement swept the nation that would change child rearing forever. 1968 Nathaniel Brandon wrote a book titled *The Psychology of Self-Esteem*. The key idea of this book is that "self-esteem" or how we evaluate our own worth was the key to a child's success. It was Brandon's thought that if a child had a high self-esteem, they would achieve highly. This book, and its ideas took off big time. Almost overnight U.S.

education policy shifted to prioritized students' self-esteem above all. In the 80's states like California formed "self-esteem task forces" that "provides us a vision for developing our human capital to make America competitive again"[62]. With this knowledge parents and teachers became extremely protective over the self-worth of their students. They became less critical of their failures, and rewarded students at every chance they could get. You'll often hear boomers say *when did kids start getting participation trophies*" this is when kids started getting participation trophies. The problem? The research was a crock of shit. 50 years and 15,000 academic studies later, the ideas have all been disproven. In fact, the self-esteem movement created a significant problem, our young people's self-worth was no longer anchored in reality. See while with good intentions, schools and parents built up their children to think they were perfect. While a child not being down on themselves is generally good, a person still needs their praise to be rooted in something they actually did. Once these kids are faced with any adversity it is so shocking that they are unable to deal with a blow to their self-worth (We are those kids by the way). Journalist Kay Hymowitz in her summary of an analysis of parenting studies stated:

> "...self-esteem doesn't improve grades, reduce anti-social behavior, deter alcohol drinking, or do much of anything good for children. In fact, telling kids how smart they are can be counterproductive. Many children who are convinced that they are little geniuses tend not to put much effort into their work."

---

[62] Kartman, Alina. "The self-esteem movement and the unhappiness of a generation." *ST Network*, 10 June 2021, https://st.network/analysis/top/the-self-esteem-movement-and-the-unhappiness-of-a-generation.html. Accessed 13 March 2024.

While the self-esteem movement has long since passed, its ideas still hold in our education system and with parents despite its failures. Thus we now have multiple generations of children who grew into adults with no idea how to build their own self-esteem. What Bronson failed to take into account is a healthy sense of self-esteem comes from the work we put into our growth. He had the order in reverse. Kids weren't doing better because they had a higher self-esteem, they had a higher self-esteem because they were doing better. A 1999 study of self-esteem and children found *"children who are praised for intelligence, not for effort, feel much more helpless when they go through a failure, because they attribute their failure to a lack of intrinsic abilities, not a lack of adequate effort"*[63]. For us this means we simply don't know how to build a proper self-image. Part of having a studier sense of self is building your self-esteem based on experiences, the majority of which are unsuccessful. We were praised for just existing for 18 years and enter the world as emotional hemophiliacs who cannot take the slightest sense of failure. Inherently though, those failures are needed for our moments of growth and our avoidance of them makes us live lives that don't reach their fullest potential emotionally or aspirationally. People should have positive thoughts about themselves, but it needs to come from something they actually did. A childhood of emotional bubble-wrap does not prepare you for adulthood, and based on current trends it barely prepares you to be a teenager. When your self-esteem isn't built on anything, you have nothing to fall back on when things don't go your way.

These dual problems spell disaster for someone trying to build a productive self-image. In parallel we live in a world which makes us constantly misjudge ourselves while not understanding how to build a

---

[63] Kartman, Alina. "The self-esteem movement and the unhappiness of a generation." ST Network, 10 June 2021, https://st.network/analysis/top/the-self-esteem-movement-and-the-unhappiness-of-a-generation.html. Accessed 13 March 2024.

self-image of value. This chapter is going to take on that problem. You're going to do what your kindergarten teacher never did for you. You're gonna learn how to take a lickin' and keep on tickin'. Part of becoming the <u>real confident you</u> is having a realistic grasp on who you are. And not in a superficial, Instagram *"oh my god I feel so seen"* way. This chapter will show you how to:

1. Decouple your identity from a superficial avatar you've created for the internet and the world.

2. Build an adequate self-identity, understand your strengths and weakness while learning to celebrate both.

A Life Unfiltered:

Do you remember the story of Narcissus? If you happened to be staring at the kid three rows away during the Greek Mythology unit in middle school here are the cliff notes. Narcissus was a handsome young Greek God. He had a terrible habit of pushing away women (Nymphs specifically?). One day these women gathered and called on the Goddess of Vengeance to get back at Narcissus for being such a narcissistic ass (yes this is where that word comes from). All the goddess had to do is show Narcissus his own reflection. So one day Narcissus leaned over a river and saw himself in the water for the first time. Narcissus fell in love with his own image. He couldn't stop looking at himself. Literally this man could not take his eyes off his own reflection. He did not eat or sleep, he just stared. Finally one day Narcissus reached out to grab his own reflection and fell in the water. Because he hadn't eaten in a week, a now withered away Narcissus drowned and died in the river.

Have you ever thought about how many pictures you have taken of yourself? If you are under 30, there has been a period of time when Snapchat was your main communication tool (or maybe it currently is). How many pictures is that solely of yourself? Every social event is now built on the picture you can get from it. And what do you do before posting? Obsessing over every detail of the photo, making sure there are no imperfections shown, or better yet removing those imperfections with a filter or facetune. We are obsessed with ourselves folks. It makes complete sense, attention is currency. The better you look, or the cooler the scenario is the more attention you get. There is a little narcissus in all of us now. Our friends expect it from us, to be "normal" means to care deeply about our own perception. This is not to say you shouldn't care what you look like. Taking pride in your appearance isn't a bad thing, but the borderline obsession we have causes us to be self-critical in ways beyond our understanding. We are in a constant search of our own flaws, and any digital or cosmetic way to fix them is adored by our following.

Am I telling you to throw your phone in the river? Of course not. But there is a better approach. When we live life for the adornment of others it does just that, pleases others. You miss the opportunity at real fulfillment, and looking back on great moments for what they actually are. Memories looked at through filters are diluted. If we set our intentions around simply wanting to remember a great moment in a photo, we don't lose that time to a self-critical and self-promotion event. Lighting sucks? Who gives a fuck. The bar you're at with your friends isn't trendy? It was fun, wasn't it. Your face looks stupid? Everyone who follows you has probably seen that face before. If people don't like what you actually look like then they don't like YOU, so fuck THEM. Do you want to live your life caring about the judgment you'll get from people at the slightest sign of authenticity? More than likely they are just projecting their own insecurities at you in an effort to feel better about their own inner narcissus. Even if your social media is your business, would it not be better to be honest with your following? When we prioritize our public avatar over ourselves we create expectations that we can't match.

A real person has bad days, and pimples, and bad hair days - all of those things are not only acceptable but should be cherished.

So how do we fix it? We set our intentions on more noble goals with our social media. Is your intention to get attention? Then you will probably do more things that will get your attention like doctoring your photos or making your entire day about taking the most flattering photo. Is your intention to highlight a great time you and your friends had because your following will enjoy it? Great! 65% of American youth report about worrying that their friends will tag them in an unattractive photo[64]. Let go, relax, and start looking at yourself for you, not the fake version of you on the internet. **Stop using filters.**

Snapchat Dysmorphia

A growing unfortunate truth is how harsh social media can be on a young woman. Men are certainly affected too in growing numbers, however, there seems to be something specifically damning for young women. Filters specifically have taken a serious toll on young women. A group already subjected to serious (and fucked up if I may add) scrutiny on their physical appearance is only amplified by doctoring photos.

Women are now going under the knife to reflect their filters. 77% of plastic surgeons reported patients coming in to get work to look "similar to their selfies"[65]. Filters are leading people to grow Body

---

[64] Piacquadio, Andrea. "What is Snapchat Dysmorphia?" *Newport Academy*, 8 October 2020, https://www.newportacademy.com/resources/empowering-teens/snapchat-dysmorphia/. Accessed 16 March 2024.

[65] AMERICAN ACADEMY OF FACIAL PLASTIC AND RECONSTRUCTIVE SURGERY, INC. "2021 Statistics & Trends Released - Demand for Facial Plastic Surgery Skyrocket." *American Academy of Facial Plastic and Reconstructive Surgery*, 10 February 2022, https://www.aafprs.org/Media/Press_Releases/2021%20Survey%20Results.aspx. Accessed 16 March 2024.

Dysmorphic Disorder (BDD). Dr. Neelam Vashi, the director of the Ethnic Skin Center at the Boston Medical Center commented[66]:

"Filtered selfies can make people lose touch with reality, creating the expectation that we are supposed to look perfectly primped all the time. A new phenomenon called 'Snapchat dysmorphia' has popped up [...] where patients are seeking out surgery to help them appear like the filtered versions of themselves."

This problem is continuing to grow as filters are being placed on us without even knowing. Did you know Zoom puts a filter on you without even asking? That's right, your work calls have a filter on them.

Cut The Legs Off Your Sweatpants:

Arnold Schwarzenegger is an iconoclast to say the least. Immigrant, bodybuilding champion, movie star and Governor of California. Aside from knocking up his maid and keeping it a secret from his wife for 16 years, the guy has lived a dream life (remember, there are no gurus, just flawed creatures doing our best). Nevertheless, the last thing many of us would think Arnold would be insecure about is his body. But when he first got to America, Arnold had one deep insecurity, his calves. This may be funny to think about, but in the world of bodybuilding the calf is no joke. When Arnold got to America it was his mission to be the greatest bodybuilder in the world. Already winning many European championships, this prodigy thought he was on the fast track to Mr. Olympia (bodybuilding's biggest prize). He was shocked when he walked into Gold's Gym for the first time and noticed the calves of all of his

---

[66] Sandoiu, Ana, and Neelam Vashi. "What is 'Snapchat dysmorphia,' and why is it concerning?" *Medical News Today*, 7 August 2018, https://www.medicalnewstoday.com/articles/322706#How-Snapchat-filters-may-affect-dysmorphia. Accessed 16 March 2024.

American contemporaries. The fear immediately struck him that his dreams would be stolen from him because of his little ankles. That night, Arnold went back to his shitty LA apartment and did the unthinkable. He cut all of his pants off at the knee. He made it impossible to hide from his problem. Every day he worked his calves and looked at them in the mirror. Now we know the rest of the story, Arnold didn't just win Mr. Olympia, but he did it seven times. With his new massive calves, he could finally wear his pants to his ankles again.

Insecurity is one of the biggest blockers to becoming <u>The Real Confident You.</u> Parents, friends, teachers, and others do you a great disservice by telling you that you are perfect. You are not perfect nor is anyone else. Imagine a world of perfect people, how boring would that be? Our uniqueness should be celebrated, for both your flaws and your strengths. Telling us, or yourself, how perfect you are all the time takes away the ability to celebrate what makes you uniquely you. It robs us of the opportunity to grow as people. There is no *"that's just the way I am"* to our personalities, we are clay and taking an active role in your molding helps you build the person that you want to see in the mirror. Accurately identifying those not-so-savory parts of yourself is hard. It's important to explore what forms us to build the version of ourselves we want to be. Let me be clear, I am not advocating beating yourself up. Every little flaw and imperfection is not meant to be picked apart. But building a healthy self-image and becoming the real confident you means facing the parts of us that we don't like and making us upset head on. There are two types of flaws that cause our insecurities, fixed and variable.

Fixed Flaws: Elements that are a part of us and cannot be changed. Typically these are physical aspects of us.

- Example: I am short as fuck. Unfortunately - I will not be having a growth spurt any time soon.

Variable Flaws: Aspects of us that can be changed.

- Example: I am an egomaniac.

For our fixed flaws, you need to just accept them. More than likely they aren't even flaws. Maybe they don't fall into traditional beauty standards, or just make you different. Flaws like these give you an experience in the world unique to you. Cherish them, don't shy away from them. These things about you that you can't change are inherently you! What a gift that is. You get to experience things in a whole new and unique way. And if someone around can't accept that, fuck them. Those judgmental assholes don't deserve to spend time with you anyway.

Our variable flaws are a little different. There are parts of our personalities and actions that are inherently us doing the wrong thing. More than likely these flaws aren't your fault, but they are something you can solve. The great part of our variable flaws is you can action them. Get too angry? Practice your breathing or read about anger management. Too judgmental of your friends? Learn how to be more empathetic. Now this is not easy, you will fail constantly. This is where you need to lean in. Failure is a perfectly fine thing in the pursuit of something noble. You can't beat yourself up for trying to do the right thing. In those failures you will learn much more about yourself than if you stood still. This constant cycle of failure you will inch a little closer to the person you want to be. You build self-esteem by being an inch better every single day, that will make you a proud person, not one shuttered by insecurity.

Flaws negatively affect our own view of yourself. It's not about the judgment of others, it's about your own self view. People can suck. Many people will judge you for simply being you. Building a positive self-image is not for other people, it's for you. Be the person you want to be, not the one the world wants. Most judgment comes from others insecurity, you can't let this form you. When taking a self-evaluation, it's important to take this into account. When picking what parts of you need improvement, do it for you.

The Network of Self Actualization:

Let's talk about your friends. We're social creatures, and going about this thing alone is impossible. We need some support along the way. There is no such thing as a self-made man. Getting by with a little help from our friends is not only a great Beatles song but an impossible task to live without. Our friends are our support, the thing that keeps us up when times aren't great. But sometimes they are not. Our friends can also be the biggest deterrent to us becoming the best versions of ourselves. Do your friends actually support you, or are they just living alongside you? Do they root for your success? Do they question the moves you make? Becoming The Real Confident You can be an isolating experience. People are easily threatened and will try to bring you down to their level because of their own insecurities or fear of your growth. It's becoming harder to tell which is which in the modern world. People will be your biggest supporter on the internet, but never root you on in real life. There are a lot of people who will comment "I am so proud of you" on a post and shit on you to their friends. Consider this a warning, if you are focusing on your growth, people will leave. You will very soon learn who those real people are. It will be painful and surprising. Hurt on the road to The Real Confident You will happen. Don't let it waiver your faith. Seek those friends that will support your growth, they will help you build a self-image that is honest and positive.

I'm Proud of You:

Has anyone told you how proud of you they are recently? Because I am proud of you. Seriously, being a human is tough business. Being hard on ourselves is our default setting. And sure, you have flaws that need work, but so does every other human walking this planet right now. When was the last time you took stock of what you're proud of? There is a lot to be proud of, we just fail to see it. Every hardship along the way got you here, and you are much better for it. Right now we're going to break out our handy dandy <u>box breathing</u>. **This time, do the exercise but set your intention on what you're proud of. Afterword, pull out your notes app and write ten things that you're proud of about yourself.** You should have practiced enough by this time to know how long you should take box breathing, but this time let's do 2 minutes.

Welcome back! I've been hard on you this chapter, I know that. I promise this isn't a Dr. Jekyll and Mr. Hyde scenario. The truth of the matter is, getting better isn't sunshine and rainbows. I wanted to finish this chapter with the pride you should have in yourself because while it's the most important part of your self-image, it's important to take it on with a certain perspective. Pride anchored in nothing leads you to not being able to actually evaluate what to be proud of. Which you have ALOT to be proud of but taking on pride with an embrace of all of your flaws gives you a balance that makes you impenetrable to self-doubt and judgment. Self-esteem is important, but it has to be grounded in reality. Yes you have problems, but god dammit you're working on it and that is AWESOME. Keep your head up kid, you're crushing it.

Chapter 6:

Touch Grass

"We are more often frightened than hurt, and we suffer more from imagination than from reality." ~ **Seneca**

We are losing grip with reality. This is not *One Flew Over the Cuckoo's Nest* or *A Beautiful Mind*, I would be ill advised to say you're seeing things. Our perception of reality though is shifting. The way we interpret the world, what we value, and our metrics of success are changing. I am not one for the culture war fodder, but there are some justifiable worries for your own sake about how you see the world. Perception is in fact reality. We have already talked about the fear economy, but what about status and sex? Both are becoming more prominent in today's culture driven by social media. I am all for the sexual revolution, but social media has done something much different. We are tying much more of our value as human beings to our image rather than our non-physical characteristics. Gen-Z is obsessed with status. Money is directly tied to your following and vice versa so wealth has more cultural cache than it ever has. These things have always been true for humans, but with social media they are blown out of proportion. Wealth is exaggerated, beauty is faked, and fear is struck constantly. If the majority of your interactions are on social media you would think the world only values you if:

1. You have wealth.

2. You are attractive or have an attractive partner (bonus points of both)

3. You align with a specific ideology and do whatever you can to fight the awful people who oppose it.

Thinking this way is a zero-sum game. There is no winning. There will always be a flaw in your looks, someone will always be richer, and most people who disagree with you are probably great people who just think differently than you. If this is how you perceive the world, there is no route to happiness. This may seem overly simple, but you need to look no further than who young people are going to for advice to find out what they think the world values and their view on reality.

Do you know who's a fucking asshole? Andrew Tate. For those of you lucky enough to be ignorant of this man, here is the gist. He and his brother Tristan grew to internet stardom in 2022 and 2023. They did so in two ways, first of which is classic internet - they said wild things they knew would go viral on their podcast and clipped them for TikTok and Instagram distribution. That's normal internet stuff, nothing too outrageous. Here is where it gets a little wild - then they created a system called "Hustlers University " where they promised commissions to people who signed up to share their videos on their feed but also they earned a higher percentage based on how many referrals a user could bring in. You do not need an MBA to understand that's a pyramid scheme. Despite this, because thousands of young boys thought they would get rich quickly from "Hustler University", Andrew Tate's videos were everywhere. Thousands of clips posted every hour from around the globe all driving traffic to one podcast.

Before "Hustlers University" was promptly shut down for being unable to deliver on its promises, these bozos were nearly unavoidable and were propelled to stardom. Their message was directed at young men, and troubling. The Tate brothers made their money previously to podcast stardom mostly by "representing" women on adult cam sites. They rented out warehouses, filled them with fake bedrooms, and put women in them working around the clock to "pleasure" men on the other side of a computer screen and took a percentage off the top of their earnings. They were virtual pimps (also they almost certainly trafficked some or all of these women which is why they are now sitting in a Romanian prison awaiting trial). How would a virtual pimp tell young men to live their lives? Be comfortable, women are evil disposable objects, and your measure of worth as a man is the figure in your bank account. Here are some actual quotes from some of the Tate brothers most viral videos:

> *"Females are the ultimate status symbol. People think I'm running around with these hoes because I like sex. That's nothing to do with the reason why I'm running around with these bitches. I got these bitches just so everyone knows who the don is."*

> *"You are exactly where you deserve to be. Change who you are and you will change how you live."*

> *"Depression isn't real. You feel sad, you move on. You will always be depressed if your life is depressing. Change it."*

> *"If you're my friend, you just can't be a pussy. 'Well, I had a heart attack', get the fuck up. Fuck's wrong with you? Go to the hospital later. Have a drink, cigarette, cup of coffee, back in the game. Fucking having heart attacks near me, you little pussy."*

You can see how his rise to fame was met with a justifiable moral panic. I cannot under stress how big this man is/was with young men. I have been a fourteen-year-old boy and let me tell you, I was dumb. This is true for young men in general who at a confused age saw/see the Tate's as role models. Ask a school teacher, every one of them has felt the influence of these men in their classrooms. Andrew Tate is not the cause of this issue, he is merely a symptom. Like a case study in modernity, we can tie many ills to his growth. We are addicted to quick fixes for complex problems. Simultaneously, we are more status driven than ever. Doing the work isn't cool, but the end result is. Ten years ago it was Dan Bilzerian, who made his fame looking like a modern Hugh Hefner, but everything was rented (including the women in his famous photos). Young people look at the world through social media and see it values money, status, and sex. For young men it means if they aren't driving a Bugatti or dating a supermodel they are worthless. And for young women it means if they don't spend every day looking like the Venus de Milo or Kim Kardasian while becoming a billionaire they are also worthless. Let me let you in on a secret ITS ALL FAKE. Social media, and our general isolationist tendencies create a worldview that is a cartoonish representation of reality. This distortion of reality manifests itself in who we seek out for guidance. The Tate brothers had a life young boys think they want, when really it's just an illusion of what they want. An oversimplified and reactionary version of the male ego, similar to the Kardashians fame with young women. And while the world on social media is completely fake, we internalize it as real. In a two-minute clip you can't cover nuance, so a race to the lowest common denominator is the only way to find success. If you consume enough internet content you begin to see it as a real-world view, and it's not just limited to the Tate brothers. Humans at large are struggling to grasp reality. Slowly as we spend more time away from the real world and in our homes we detach ourselves from reality. This detachment from reality is evidenced in many social behaviors that are ticking up in large numbers:

Politics Divisiveness: Our political system is polarized because of the need for good guy versus bad guy narratives as opposed to issue driven discourse. Politicians are finding more frequent success in demonizing their opponents as opposed to presenting a plan. It is much easier to have someone to blame for all of your problems and sell that on social media versus engaging in actual ideas.

Pornography: Young men (and surprisingly young women) are watching porn at an alarming rate. Part of this is clearly due to ease of access, especially for young teens (73% of 13–17-year-olds watch porn, and 54% saw it first before they turned 13)[67]. But also, due to the objectification inherent in social media, sex itself is becoming commoditized. Social media drives us to look at each other of pieces of meat to trade for status. We are looking at each other as objects, not people.

Shrinking Human Interactions and Networks: On average since the pandemic, the average person's personal or professional networks has shrunk by 16%[68]. We generally fear each other much more. 70% of Americans have low trust in each other Americans, a number that has grown significantly in 20 years[69]. Of course we don't trust each other, you can and do see every maniac in the world every night on your phone even though a person like that really only represents half a percent of the population. Helicopter parenting has made kids grow up with a fear of the outside world, and social media and the news is doing the same for adults.

Credit Card Debt and Young People: The rat race for status is driving a troubling trend for young people. Gez-Z is accumulating credit card debt faster than any American generation in history[70]. The need to keep up with the internet joneses is leading to unrealistic expectations of wealth and possessions.

---

[67] Common Sense Media. "New Report Reveals Truths About How Teens Engage with Pornography." *PR Newswire*, 10 January 2023, https://www.prnewswire.com/news-releases/new-report-reveals-truths-about-how-teens-engage-with-pornography-301717607.html. Accessed 18 March 2024.

[68] King, Marissa, and Balaza Kovacs. "Research: We're Losing Touch with Our Networks." *Harvard Business Review*, 12 February 2021, https://hbr.org/2021/02/research-were-losing-touch-with-our-networks. Accessed 18 March 2024.

[69] Pew Research. "Americans' trust in other Americans." *Pew Research Center*, 22 July 2019, https://www.pewresearch.org/politics/2019/07/22/the-state-of-personal-trust/. Accessed 18 March 2024.

[70] Business Insider. "Gen Z Is Accumulating Credit Card Debt Faster Than Other Gens: Report." *Business Insider*, 22 March 2023, https://www.businessinsider.com/gen-z-rack-up-credit-card-debt-faster-millennials-genx-2023-3. Accessed 18 March 2024.

We're losing touch. It's incredibly hard to be <u>The Real Confident You</u> without a firm grip on the world around you. Being scared, objectifying love, being driven only by status, and demonizing all that disagree with you does not make <u>The Real Confident You.</u> This kind of worldview does not lead to love and kindness, to yourself or others. In this chapter I will address how to get back in touch with reality. Getting to the <u>The Real Confident You</u> involves changing your view of the world. As a 16-year-old, I put up a fake persona to match my fake view of reality. In dissolving my fake reality I found it much easier to approach the world in a real way. How did I do that? Let's take a look:

Literally Touch Grass:

Go outside and be in nature. We are not meant to be indoors all day. Literally sheltering our existence traps us in our thoughts and stresses. Not leaving the world outside your window causes you to lose touch with it. Spending regular time outdoors resets your perspective to a realistic view of the world. Also, our physical bodies set many of our regulatory systems around the outdoors and not going outside knocks many of those out of whack. Spending just 90 minutes in nature a week has been shown to:

1. Better your breathing.

2. Improve your sleep.

3. Reduce depression and increase feelings of emotional wellbeing.

4. Reduce overall levels of stimulation, leading to a more relaxed state.

Thanks to Teddy Roosevelt, we are one of the few nations with tons of protected green space in and out of cities. Use it.

Talk to people in real life:

People do not act as they do on the internet. Also, those that talk the most are not representative of the larger population. Having conversations with people in real life will keep you in constant surprise. We need to feel connected to people to be safe, and social media gives the illusion of that but not the actual effects. The American Psychological Association found conversations with strangers give us stronger feelings of connectedness and wellbeing than those on social media[71]. I also understand that many of us struggle with social anxiety. And even if you don't, expanding your social group is hard. Here are some really easy ways to spend time with actual people conversing more often:

1. **Find groups with similar interests**: There are groups all over your local area that meet regularly, join them. Like video games? Join a club. Like books? Join a book club (and promote this book please, I have to eat). One of the great things about the modern world is we can celebrate our niches, use what you like to your advantage. Plus, it's much easier to start a conversation with someone you don't know if you already have something in common.

2. **Don't dismiss people you disagree with:** Be honest, we are a little sensitive as a generation. We are extremely likely to exclude people that don't align with us politically or otherwise. Don't do that. You are missing an opportunity to humanize the opposition and maybe learn a new perspective. It's much harder to hate or be scared of a group when you call someone in that group a friend. Plus, you're just limiting your at-bats.

---

[71] American Psychological Association. "Getting beyond small talk: Study finds people enjoy deep conversations with strangers." *American Psychological Association*, 30 September 2021, https://www.apa.org/news/press/releases/2021/09/deep-conversations-strangers. Accessed 19 March 2024.

3. **Volunteer:** There is no better feeling than doing something for someone else. Plus, you can almost guarantee that the people you meet at a volunteer organization are kind and open minded. Our communities need a lot of help. There's no reason it can't benefit you to help others.

4. **Find professional groups in your area:** First of all, this is just a good idea, mental health or otherwise, there is nothing that will help you more than your network. Similarly, people love to talk about work. Advance your career and your mental health.

5. **Be the person that sets the time with your friends:** Does nothing ever leave the group chat with your friends? You can be the one to change that. If you set a date and force the issue, people show up. Yes they may hate you on the drive to whatever you're doing, but they will thank you later. It's like Field of Dreams, if you build a social event, they will come.

6. **Stop saying no:** Have you ever seen the movie *Yes Man* with Jim Carrey? That's you now. Stop saying no to things because you're too tired or scared. Make memories, don't run from them.

Hippie shit that works:

Listen, I wear Birkenstocks, I have a vinyl collection, and my indie rock phase was very real. Have you seen the glasses I'm wearing on the back cover of this book? You get who I am, I like some hippie shit. Crystals, astrology, etc., most of its garbage. But the hippies have a few things right. They are the most connected and happy people you'll meet. I am not talking about lives on daddy's trust fund and wearing tie dyes while taking ecstasy at music festival hippies. I am talking about lives in a van that is completely detached from society hippies. No, this is not the part of the book where I try to convince you to abandon all possessions and embrace buddha. I feel the need to highlight some of the things these beautiful dirtballs do to feel better connected to the world around them because some of it is seriously helpful for gaining a healthy connection to the world around you:

1. **Yoga**: A bunch of dudes just got real defensive seeing this word. Listen, almost every professional athlete does yoga now, you can too. The main benefit of yoga in this context beyond its ability to teach you how to destimulate is connecting with your body. Also it consistently scores better than almost every other technique in reducing anxiety and depression, sharpening your brain and increasing your mood[72]. The breath to movement nature of Yoga allows you to reconnect with your body in ways most movement can't. It's not mysticism, being better connected to your body makes you feel safer and more confident.

2. **Know where your food comes from:** How often when you are at the grocery store do you think about where that food came from? The number of people I have come across who oppose hunting but feel perfectly comfortable buying a pack of ground beef in a cellophane wrapper is ridiculous. Going to things like farmers markets or butcher shops lets you gain a better understanding of where your food is coming from and the people behind it. You will gain a higher appreciation for your dinner when you shake the hand of the farmer or butcher who did the work.

3. **Take pride in the trees man:** Pick up the trash you see on the ground. When you take responsibility for the world around you it gives you a much better connectedness and respect for it and yourself. Earth is your home, pick up your mess. You'll feel good for it.

---

[72] Harvard Medical School. "Yoga for better mental health." *Harvard Health*, 12 June 2021, https://www.health.harvard.edu/staying-healthy/yoga-for-better-mental-health. Accessed 19 March 2024.

Actually yes, new friends:

DJ Khaled, Drake, and Rick Ross in 2013 released their summer smash hit song *"No New Friends"* and it went like this:

"No new friends, no new friends

No new friends, no, no, new"

You get the gist and it's dumb. Yes you should absolutely make new friends. Think about all the perspectives you're missing? Talking to people who are only like you is not only boring, it's regressive. Expand your horizons a little bit. Stop judging people before you have even met them. Let the world surprise you. When you made friends as a kid was everyone the same or did you just all happen to be on the playground? Even if you took a real look at your friends now, I bet they aren't all the same. But at some point you shut out the possibility of engaging with new people. There is a big and beautiful world out there, and you're missing the opportunity to connect with it when you shut most of it down. Try new things, meet new people, hold your judgment, and watch a waterfall of new joys enter.

Stop Doordashing:

Getting what you want instantly is convenient, but is it good for you? We are all forgoing going out to eat, shopping, and getting groceries for the convenience of doing it on our phone. Does it take more time to go to the grocery store and actually pick out the vegetables yourself versus getting it on Instacart? Sure, but spending the entire day inside is not optimal. We lose the feeling of satisfaction of a job well done when we let go of our responsibilities to our internet overlords. Amazon bringing everything you could ever need to your house in a day is a miracle, but you are missing an opportunity to go out and do something. Shopping may seem mundane, but doing things for yourself is an essential part of the human experience you miss out on when you order through a delivery app. When you can, go to the store, go out to eat, and experience life. The little moments in the world are when the best surprises come.

Identitarianism:

When you think you are at war, you will value your tribe above all. Most issues in modernity are simplified to good guy versus bad guy. When you think those that oppose you are evil you will do anything to justify beating them. That's where we have landed politically and socially. Identitarianism, or the idea that you should put your identity (specifically race, gender, political association, etc.) at the forefront of your perspective of the world. This kind of thinking has captured the fringes of American politics and of how we interact socially. On the right, it's a more classic case like in Charleston Virginia at the *"Unite the Right"* rally when white supremacists gathered (remember those pieces of shit holding tiki torches?) chanting things like "the Jews will not replace us". While this is completely vile, I don't think I need to explain racism or why it's wrong to you. On the left there is a different kind of identitarian ideology taking form, one that while may have good intentions, could have some devastating results. The left's identitarianism is obsessed with oppressor versus oppressed. Being a victim comes with a certain amount of cultural cache, and anyone deemed as an oppressor should be shunned from society. Jonathan Haight, NYU Professor, social psychologist, and best-selling author talked about on a podcast episode seeing the rise of identitarianism on college campuses[73]:

---

[73] Haidt, Jonathan. "#2121 - Jonathan Haidt The Joe Rogan Experience." *Wikipedia*, https://podcasts.apple.com/us/podcast/2121-jonathan-haidt/id360084272?i=1000649738432. Accessed 20 March 2024.

"That brings us to the issue of Identitarianism, which I think is a of what's happened on campus is the move to focus on identity as the primary analytical lens in a number of disciplines, not in most disciplines, but in a lot of humanities, and the social studies departments. So by putting identity first and then ranking identities you are saying some identities are good some are bad. This really activates our ancient tribalism, and liberal tradition going back hundreds of years is really an attempt to push back against that and to create an environment in which we can all get along. And so, as I see it from inside the academy, we've always been interested in identity. It's an important topic. There's a lot of research on it going back many decades. But something happened in 2015 on campus that really elevated Identitarianism into the dominant paradigm, not dominant in that most people believed it. But dominant in the sense that if you go against it, you're going to be destroyed socially."

Most of us are not this extreme. If you're reading this I will assume you aren't a racist or an identity obsessed Marxist. Like most of the issues we have discussed in this book, this kind of identitarianism does not manifest itself in extreme politics for the average person. But we are growing deeper into our niches. Our music tastes, fashion, tv and movies have all become more fractured along identity lines. For previous generations, there were shared cultural moments that could more easily connect people who didn't share the same outward facing identity. Take for instance TV, in 1983 the show *M*A*S*H*'s finale 106 million people tuned in to see the end of the universally beloved show[74]. Now a similar

---

[74] Cotter, Padraig. "Why MASH's Finale Is Still The Most Watched TV Episode Of All Time." *Screen Rant*, 24 September 2022, https://screenrant.com/mash-show-finale-most-viewed-tv-episode/. Accessed 20 March 2024.

nighttime comedy is lucky to get 3 million viewers[75]. Because we have a much wider variety of options we are more likely to choose things that are the most like us, fracturing our cultural identity. We lack universal shared cultural experiences which leads us to distrust each other. We keep people out of our lives who aren't similar to us in enough categories because we find them dangerous or different.

There is fragility in not having your worldview expanded. For you to have a healthy perspective of reality, you have to have actually experienced it. Most people are well intentioned, stepping out of your cultural box will let you see that. Our differences should be celebrated, not something we fear in each other. We have way more in common then we don't, opening your mind up to the world lets you see that. You'll find the world to be a comfortable place when you think it's not out to get you. The thing you should identify with most is that you are human. Are you an urbanite from Brooklyn? Talk to a farmer, they are the sweetest people you'll ever meet. Are you an oil rigger? Go to the city and talk to some people, they're not so different at all.

Put Your Robes Down

Daryl Davis is not your typical blues musician. For the last 30 years, Daryl a black man, has been befriending members of the KKK. It started 30 years ago, after a set at a small venue he sat down at the bar. Man sat next to him to talk to him about how he liked his music. After a bit of conversation this white man admitted this was the first time he had ever spoken with a black man. Later in the conversation, he admitted he was a member of the Ku Klux Klan. Despite the white man being part of an organization built on hating people who looked like

---

[75] Webb, Matt. "'FBI' and 'International' Most-Watched TV Shows Tuesday." *TVLine*, 13 March 2024, https://tvline.com/ratings/password-season-2-premiere-viewers-nbc-1235187556/. Accessed 20 March 2024.

Daryl, they were able to bond over music. The white man started coming to all Daryl's shows. Eventually the white man handed over his Klan robes, left the organization and is still a lifelong friend of Daryl's. Daryl knew he was on to something and began seeking out members across the country.

30 years later Daryl has convinced more than 200 Klan members to give him their robes and leave the KKK. It's much harder to hate when you make a friend. Aside from Daryl being a hero we should all aspire to be, there is something we should take into our everyday lives. We are all able to change with a little exposure and a friend.

You hit the jackpot, act like it:

Do you know how lucky you are? By all accounts you are living in the greatest, freest, and easiest time to be a human ever. Here he goes again rattling off stats:

If your household makes $10,000 a year you are richer than 80% of the world, if your family makes $50,000 you are in the richest 99%[76].

Life expectancy is the highest it has been in human history[77].

You are alive after the industrial revolution, almost everything you do, see or touch was not possible 150 years ago.

There are hundreds more reasons why you should be thankful to be alive today. Does America have its problems? Tons. But frankly, so does the

---

[76] Hovde, Elizabeth. "Income in perspective: America's poor are among the world's wealthy." *Oregon Live*, 4 August 2012, https://www.oregonlive.com/hovde/2012/08/income_in_perspective_americas.html. Accessed 19 March 2024.

[77] Ortiz, Esteban, and Max Roser. "Happiness and Life Satisfaction." *Our World in Data*, https://ourworldindata.org/happiness-and-life-satisfaction. Accessed 19 March 2024.

rest of the world and our problems are significantly easier than any other civilization had to face. For god's sake, we have so much food that our problem is obesity not starvation. A mountain dew would have put a Victorian child in a coma, and now you have modern medicine which can save your life in 99% of scenarios. Of all the humans ever born you are one of the luckiest,

Many would like you to believe you have a lot to be worried about, which is true. But that doesn't outweigh how much you have to be thankful for. Practice that gratitude and you will see the world in a much different light. Zoom out, life is good.

You at 80:

You will be old someday. On some deep level we have a hard time letting ourselves believe that, but it's true. Societally we treat our elderly awfully, and it's partially due to our own fear of aging. However, someday you will be on the front porch on your rocking chair, what will you think? Will you think of all the time spent in your house? I'm gonna assume not. You'll think of the memories made out in the world. If this chapter has one message it's GET OUT THERE. You can't find enjoyment if you aren't seeking it.

Chapter 7:

Be Comfortable Being Uncomfortable

---

*"The way I see it, if you want the rainbow,
you gotta put up with the rain."* ~ **Dolly Parton**

If I were to get a rib tattoo kinda guy, it would say the phrase *"Be Comfortable Being Uncomfortable"* permanently inked on me. This is the phrase that changed and saved my life. Kids, life's hard. Big deal. It's not fair ever. Adversity is pretty much the only consistent thing in human life. Facing it with joy and using it to benefit you is what creates The Real Confident You. Up to this point I bet you have faced a lot of adversity. Maybe it was your childhood, grief of a lost loved one, struggle with your own identity, career failure or trauma. Have those adversities shaped you? I bet they made you who you are. Having control in that shaping is what I am going to try to teach you here. You are accountable for how adversity affects you. Good news, you are in complete control. Bad news, it's a painful skill to learn.

We've heard all the cliches, Oprah was fired from her first TV gig, Michael Jordan was cut from his high school basketball team, Tom Brady was benched in college, Steve Jobs was a college dropout etc. Trials and tribulations are on the horizon my friend, and you need to learn how to use them to your advantage. Let me let you in on a secret I found out in the business world, everyone is faking it until they figure it out. I spent the first year of my career on the phone with CEO's who were constantly seeking help and advice. No one has it all figured out, and the only way to get better is to seek the unknown and work your way through it. Now I am not suggesting that you should be a fake, but putting yourself in situations you have never been in before or are uncomfortable is the only way to grow. And in that growth, you will find the strengths you have to get whatever you want in this life. Take for instance, Dwayne "The

Rock" Johnson. We all know him now as a movie star, pro wrestling phenom, and the brand face of every brand Kevin Hart and Shaq have turned down.

In 1996 Dwayne was staring down the failure of his football career. As a highly sought after college prospect Dwayne took his talents to the University of Miami, despite the team's success (including a national championship in 1991), Dwayne was plagued with injuries and barely saw the field as a starter. He then set his sights on the NFL, but in the 1995 NFL Draft no team wanted to take a shot on a player with the minimal resume Dwayne had in college. So, taking the only opportunity he had, Dwayne signed with the Calgary Stampeders, a team in the Canadian Football League. If being forced to play for no money in a league no one watched wasn't bad enough, Dwayne was cut from Calgary in his first season with the team. So now Dwayne had no options, looking down into his wallet he saw $7 which was the only money to his name. With his back against the wall Dwayne decided to join the family business. Professional Wrestling. Dwayne's dad Rocky Johnson was a long-time professional wrestler and crowd favorite. When pursuing his father for a job he was met with hesitation (actually he and his dad had a knock down drag out fight about it). But convinced Dwayne was serious Rocky took on training his son. After 3 months Dwayne made a call to Pat Patterson, a VP at the WWF (now WWE). Pat came to see Dwayne workout and invited him to WWE's National Televised weekly show Monday Night Raw for a tryout match. His first Pro Wrestling Match ever would be in front of 15,000 people in Corpus Christi Texas. Dwayne performed well in his first match and was pulled aside by WWF Founder and CEO Vince McMahon. Vince liked Dwayne, but needed to see more, so he booked him for a "house show" (a non-televised WWF event) the next day. Dwayne performed well again, but not well enough for Vince's liking. So Vince sent Dwayne to a much smaller wrestling promotion in Tennessee to hone his skills. After taking fake punches and throwing himself through tables in front of twenty people in high school gyms in Tennessee for a few months, Vince called. His message, it was time for Dwayne's big break. In Madison Square Garden Dwayne with his new stage name "Rocky Mavia" was premiering at the WWF's pay-per-view event "Royal Rumble". Not just that, he was slated to win the main event. Before I go further I have to explain something about the wrestling world. Yes it's fake, but how they decide who wins is completely fan driven. It's a tickets, merch, and pay-per-view event driven business. It's essentially a soap opera in spandex. The people who the fans like get the big bucks, win the "championships", and keep a job. The fans did not like Rocky Mavia. Dwayne's character was supposed to be the ultimate good guy, constantly smiling and being respectful. Here's the problem, bad guys were all the rage. Not long after his start with the WWF Dwayne would come out to "Rocky Sucks" chants through his entire match. The shooting star couldn't even leave the sky. Vince was not happy and made it clear Dwayne was going to lose his job. To make matters worse he injured his knee and had to take time off. After recovering Vince made it clear his next appearance on Monday Night Raw may be his last shot. Dwayne asked for two things in his last crack at the bat, to play a bad guy and for two minutes with a microphone. The bad guy part was a no brainer, but it took extra pleading to give the microphone to Dwayne with no experience. Now going by The Rock, he made an impassioned bad guy speech lashing out at the fans for booing him and seemingly every doubter along the way. It took his last chance with his back against the wall to find out, "The Rock" had a natural talent behind the microphone. The fans loved it. For the first time he showed his biggest talent, his mouth. Instead of a fake smile he spoke the truth, he found <u>the real confident him</u>. After two months he was the most popular wrestler in the WWF. 20+ years later, he is now widely recognized as one of the best to ever do it.

We all know what "The Rock" is now. His production company "Seven Bucks Productions" (a nod to that day he was cut from Calgary) has grossed $4.6 Billion dollars at the box office. Not bad for a washed-up backup? Most of us in that scenario would be left to a life of destitution, but because Dwayne embraced the discomfort he learned what would be the signature element of his career. There were dozens of big failures and hundreds of little ones on the way to Dwayne becoming "The Rock". In each of those were lessons that he took to become the megastar we all know. *"Pat I don't have huge muscles or a dad to get me in a lucrative business"* - I get it. Being on your last leg is not the only way to find the <u>real confident you.</u> However, avoiding the things that will be uncomfortable to us has us miss the opportunity to grow and find what will make us the <u>real confident you.</u> Creating those situations in small doses is how we grow and find our own strengths. In this chapter I will teach not only how to lean into that discomfort but seek it. Most importantly, I will go over how to deal with it and use it as a tool to better yourself.

There is a lot of suck in there, but he embraced it and persevered.

The Virtue of Lifelong Learning

Part of becoming <u>The Real Confident You</u> is learning. About yourself and the world. To do this correctly you need to understand how you learn. Being able to learn well is a skill of its own. Society has taught you that things in your academic or career life you are not good at or have trouble picking up certain things because of your ability. While this is partially true, the much more likely scenario is you don't know how you learn in the best way for success. I am not just talking about accumulating information for a school test either. Knowledge and wisdom are formed from a life of learning, when you stop learning you stop growing. We have all come across a middle-aged person who is stuck in their youth. Bowling for Soup certainly covered this ground in that *1985* song. At some point in life, people give up on learning and growing. For eternity they are locked into being the person they were in college, or the big high school football star. Their music doesn't evolve, their views don't evolve and subsequently they don't evolve. Becoming <u>The Real Confident You</u> involves the opposite. You need to constantly learn and change into a better version of you every day. So how do you learn? Well that is different for every person.

Each of us learns differently. One of the biggest disadvantages of the American school system is this isn't often taken into account. For you to take on life's lessons out of the classroom, you will need to know how you learn. Luckily, most of us can be segmented into certain learning styles. You will probably not just fall in one of these learning styles but multiple. The four main styles of learner are[78]:

---

[78] VARK. "The VARK Modalities: Visual, Aural, Read/write & Kinesthetic." *VARK Learning*, https://vark-learn.com/introduction-to-vark/the-vark-modalities/. Accessed 25 March 2024.

1. **Visual** - An individual who favors visual learning tends to prefer observing and perceiving information through visuals such as pictures, diagrams, written instructions, and other graphical representations. This learning style is often labeled as "spatial" learning. People who excel in visual learning comprehend information more effectively when it is presented visually. As a student this person enjoys doodling, making lists, and taking detailed notes.

2. **Auditory** - Auditory learners learn best when information is reinforced through sound. They prefer listening to lectures rather than reading notes, often using their own voices to understand new concepts. These learners prefer reading aloud and are comfortable speaking in class, excelling at verbal explanations. They may read more slowly and repeat information given by teachers.

3. **Kinesthetic** - Kinesthetic learners, also known as tactile learners, acquire knowledge through hands-on experiences or physical activities. They prefer engaging in actions such as acting out events or using their hands to touch and manipulate objects to comprehend concepts better. These learners may find it challenging to remain seated for long periods and often excel in sports or enjoy activities like dancing. They may require more frequent breaks during study sessions.

4. **Reading/Writing** - Reading/writing learners favor learning through written words. Although there is some similarity with visual learning, these learners are specifically attracted to expressing themselves through writing, reading articles or books, keeping diaries, consulting dictionaries for word meanings, and using the internet extensively for research purposes.

Often you will hear college juniors say, *"I like college better than high school because I do most of the learning on my own"*. These people were given the opportunity to understand which learning style led to their most successful grades and repeated it. For you, how do you know which style of learner you are? Well, let's take a look at your hobbies. We think of our hobbies as just things we like to do, but often they are emblematic of what comes most naturally to us.

There is an idea that reinforces this called *"The Swimmers Body Fallacy"*. It is meant to show how we often confuse selection criteria with results. Let's say it's the Summer Olympics and you turn on a swimming competition. Observing numerous swimmers might lead one to believe that swimming is responsible for producing great bodies. Consequently, if one aims to achieve a great physique, they might consider taking up swimming, given that exceptional swimmers often exhibit impressive physical attributes (Micheal Phelps is shredded).

While it's common to believe that swimming leads to the development of great bodies, the reality is that top swimmers often already possess great bodies, which contribute significantly to their success in the sport. This is *"The Swimmers Body Fallacy"* people don't often get great bodies because they swim, they have great bodies, so they swim. The first time they got in the pool they were more than likely already better and more gifted than anyone at their elementary school, so they found enjoyment in it and kept going.

With that in mind we often choose to do things for fun we are naturally inclined to do. If you like pottery for instance, you probably do so because you have some natural ability at it. Our innate abilities are the easiest place to fill out our curiosities and attention spans. So if we compare our hobbies to learning styles we can get a comprehensive understanding of what learning styles we fall into.

What's my learning style quiz?

You will learn best bydoing the things you naturally enjoy. If we take a look at what you do for fun, we can probably guess what your learning style is. Take a look at the hobbies of each learning style, they typically match with the characteristics of the style.

Visual:	Auditory
• Movies	• Music
• TV	• Podcasts
• Attending sporting events	• Lectures
• Appreciating visual art	• Discussions/Debates
• Graphically impressive video games	• Documentaries
• Drawing	
Kinesthetic	Reading/Writing
• Exercise/Sports	• Books
• Dancing	• Newspapers
• Crafts	• Journaling
• Yardwork/Home Improvement	• Story Driven Video Games
• High Action Video Games	

Obviously, there are many more hobbies that fit in these buckets, but you understand my point. More than likely, what you do for fun falls in a couple of these categories, great! This means you probably fall into those learning styles. If you are still a little confused as to where you fall, examine why you like the hobbies you do. Take for instance cooking. If you like to cook because you enjoy the physical process, you are probably a kinesthetic learner. If you like cooking because you enjoy the presentation of the plate, you are more likely a visual learner.

Now this doesn't mean you avoid subjects or disciplines that don't apply to your learning model directly, instead modify it to fit your needs. For instance, I am primarily an auditory learner. Naturally, I read very slowly. Reading is not a hobby that comes naturally to me. However when the stat "Most CEO's read 52 books a year and the average employee reads 1" was constantly thrown in my face (which I can't find anywhere to validate but is thrown around at cocktail parties like it's the 10 fucking commandments). I knew I had to read more.

Given that I am an auditory learner, to pick up my reading skill I listened to an audiobook while following the words on the page of the same book. I did this with a couple books until I could take the audiobook training wheels off. Then I acted as if I was reading aloud in my head (strange to think about but I bet you are doing it right now you just aren't conscious of it). In 2023 I read 80 books after not reading an entire book all the way through my high school career (sorry Ms. Karls I lied on those To Kill a Mockingbird tests, read it this year though - it's amazing). This applies to anything. You are capable of whatever you want, lean on your natural strengths to accomplish it.

"Great Pat, I can do better on a chemistry test, how does this affect my life?" We are constantly learning. It's the only way to improve. These skills can be applied to learning about yourself. There are a million self-care activities to do, the ones that will work for you likely match how you learn. People are dogmatic about self-care, but it's not one size fits all.

More importantly you need to constantly challenge your current knowledge of the world. To grow as a person, your ideas need to grow with it. Exposure is power, and learning is freedom. Want to be more comfortable in the world? Learn about it. If you have an opinion you think can't be challenged, challenge it. Those "aha" moments we deprive ourselves of leave us mentally sedated. Want to know the truth about me being at least mentally healthy? I thought I knew everything. It was only when I realized how little I knew that I was able to grow. Knowledge is like a fish in a tank, it will only grow to the size of the glass. You set the size of the glass in your head. *"It's too hard ... I'm not good at it"*. Bullshit. Socrates said, **"Smart people learn from everything and everyone, average people from their experiences, stupid people already have all the answers."**. You are capable of anything and can learn ANYTHING. It's the age of information, you can get a college degree's worth of knowledge on your phone in two weeks. The more you learn, the better you get at it. Being curious and constantly learning makes you nimbler in life. You can adjust to changes quicker, be more empathic, and have an enriched perspective. Transforming into <u>The Real Confident You</u> is much easier when you are more adaptable.

If you are going through a hard time and you are a kinesthetic learner, journaling about your issues probably won't be your best option. But going on a run or taking an art class will present you with the answers you are looking for. Getting to know how your brain works will give you something to fall back on when you fail or times are tough. Knowing your natural strengths helps form an identity that can take on anything.

The knowledge that you can teach yourself is a superpower in any hardship.

You don't just need to understand how you learn, you need to practice it. Given the importance of standardized testing, much work has been done to see which study habits are the most effective. The resounding answer is taking practice tests. Those who take practice tests are not only learning subject matter, but the skill of taking a test. The only way to learn that skill is to try repeatedly and learn from your mistakes. Sometimes it takes a student three or four tries to get a question in a practice test, but that student will not likely get a similar test wrong in the real scenario. We learn best when we repeat our actions. Additionally, exposing ourselves to uncomfortable scenarios repeatedly makes them more tolerable. After all, it's much easier to take a test after you have practiced it 30 times. Wish I knew this when I took my ACT. I walked in having spammed flashcards for exactly one night with a sweat that would make a southern Baptist preacher jealous. To learn and improve, you have to practice. The thing that is holding you back most probably is not your skill, it's your fear of failure. Let's hold that thought for the next section.

Frederick Douglas Schoolhouse Freedom

There is nothing more empowering than knowledge. No people in human history know this more than slaves, especially Fredrick Douglass. Douglass was born into slavery in the American south in 1818. The practice at the time was to purposely make sure slaves stayed uneducated. Not just because it was socially frowned upon but because it was illegal. Keeping a slave under your thumb as a slave master was much easier if they had no knowledge of the outside world. Elias B. Caldwell, clerk of the Supreme Court of the United states in the early 1800s said this about keeping slaves uneducated:

---

*"The more you improve the condition of these people, the more
you cultivate their minds, the more miserable you make them,
in their present state. You give them a higher relish for those
privileges which they can never attain, and turn what we
intend for a blessing [slavery] into a curse. No, if they must
remain in their present situation, keep them in the lowest state
of degradation and ignorance. The nearer you bring them to
the condition of brutes, the better chance do you give them of
possessing their apathy."*

Sick and twisted for sure, but an effective strategy to keep people under your control. If you want people to accept their current state in life, don't let them know there is any other way (read Plato's *Allegory of The Cave*). Luckily for Frederick and all of us, one of his slave masters did not follow the law. In his young life (around age 6) one of his slave masters Sophia Auld took a liking to Frederick. She taught him the alphabet and how to read. Additionally, unlike most slaves he lived near Baltimore where he got to see not only other slaves, but free black people. Exposure was everything. Sophia's husband did not approve of Fredericks education and eventually got Sophia to stop. This included hiding all reading materials and punishment (whipping) if Frederick was caught trying to read. This did not stop Fredrick, who continued to read anything he could find even as he was sent off to two other slave masters. He eventually escaped slavery using his smarts to act as a freeman including varying costumes and playing characters he read about to take trains to New York City where slavery was illegal.

We all owe a great debt to the education Frederick sought while enslaved. Once a freeman, he fought against slavery. His works were some of the most influential in the country. His newspaper "The North Star", speeches, and books were widely influential, and get wide credit in ending slavery in the United States. His works had much effect on Abraham Lincoln whom he met with during the civil war (historians I get I am overly simplifying this, I only can hold attention about a guy from the 1850's for so long).

Knowledge was not only what freed him and helped Frederick free every slave in the country, it's what allowed it to happen. Both from good old-fashioned books and seeing the world Frederick formed a strength many of us will never know. When Frederick Douglas said *"knowledge is the pathway from slavery to freedom"* he didn't just mean people in chains. He meant that his education gave him a liberated mind. Slave owners weren't scared of an educated slave because they may read a lock picking book, their fear was because a free thinker is the most powerful tool in the world. When I was a kid I read a quote of Fredericks at a Civil War museum I think of often:

"Education means emancipation. It means light and liberty. It means the uplifting of the soul of man into the glorious light of truth, the light by which men can only be made free."

Slavery didn't end with the last shot of the civil war, it ended when the enslaved could liberate their minds. Don't take for granted your freedom to learn. The world has given you more opportunity to be your best self than any time in human history. Be thankful for that. Frederick Douglas had to hide in the middle of the night to read and if he was caught would be whipped. You on the other hand have unlimited information at your fingertips. You will face many challenges in this life. However, becoming a lifelong learner is your best ticket to freedom. That kind of freedom is the greatest confidence builder in the world. You know how much confidence Frederick Douglas had to speak openly about ending slavery as a black man in

1859? We should be lucky to have an ounce of that. The only way to achieve that self-belief is to know the world you navigate. Lastly, you are never too smart to keep learning. If you think something can't be questioned, question it. If something doesn't make sense, follow your instinct, and dig in. Don't ever let your fear of seeming stupid override your ability to learn. Frederick Douglass's contemporary Booker T. Washington said:

"Never get to the point where you will be ashamed to ask anybody for information. The ignorant man will always be ignorant if he fears that by asking another for information he will display ignorance. Better once display your ignorance of a certain subject than always know nothing of it."

Fear of Failure

Being scared of failure is an epidemic. News flash, you're gonna fuck up. You're gonna fuck up more than you don't. Guess what, so is every other human on Earth, stop fearing it.

In 1974 Fleetwood Mac had already released ten albums. Not a single one of them was successful. In fact, they had failed miserably. The band had broken up, fired members, rehired original members, sued each other and moved from England to the United States. They realized with the failures of their first ten albums they would need a pop sensibility to keep the band alive. So they looked for new members. After adding Christie McVie earlier in the decade, Fleetwood Mac found the final pieces of their shifting band puzzle when they met a young couple named Stevie Nicks and Lindsay Buckingham. With their newly formed sound and drama free (for now) band in place, they wrote an album that would change the world. Given the name, many assume it's the band's first album, but *Fleetwood Mac* was their 11th and its waves in music are still felt today. With hits like *"Rhiannon"* and *"Landslide"* (your mom for sure played this in the car) the album went 4x platinum. They didn't just save the band, they were megastars. Their success would soon be topped by their next album *Rumors* (which is a wild album basically about all of the band members cheating on each other with other members of the band). Despite being released in 1977, *Rumors* still routinely hits the Billboard charts, a rarity for any album, let alone one that is nearing 50 years old. *"Dreams"* and *"The Chain"* off of the album both have over a billion streams on Spotify, a feat most modern artists could only dream of. In 2020 *"Dreams"* had another run as a number one song in America after a TikTok went viral of a man singing it while riding his skateboard drinking cranberry juice (that guy was so chill). All of this success could never have happened if they were scared to keep going.

After 10 albums most people give up. Think about the guy from your hometown that put out raps on SoundCloud. Fleetwood Mac didn't. With each failure they got closer to their goals. It took ten huge failures to realize what they were missing. Approach your life the same way. At NASA they don't even use the word failure, instead they say, "early attempts at success"[79]. Failure isn't a bad thing, stop treating it like it. Most of us are paralyzed in fear to get what we want. I suffer from it as much as anybody, but in becoming the real confident me I knew to reach the goals I had you just have to try and probably fail. And even though I failed I could take what I learned from those failures in my next attempt.

Our brains are naturally risk averse. It made sense for your ancestors. Most of the fools who rushed in without a care in the world of failing a new hunting technique died in the teeth of a saber tooth tiger and did not pass down their genes (except to the Jackass guys). When you don't expose yourself to enough potential failure, it feels as serious as death.

---

[79] Myers, Mike. "Quote by Mike Myers: "In fact, NASA doesn't use the F-word; instead, ...""" *Goodreads*, https://www.goodreads.com/quotes/8333725-in-fact-nasa-doesn-t-use-the-f-word-instead-they-call. Accessed 27 March 2024

But it's something we can and should build a tolerance for. Utilizing our neuroplasticity if we repeatedly expose ourselves to the potential of failing our tolerance for it goes up. We are wired to not want to fail, but what's truer is we are wired to get used to hard tasks. Remember the first time you drove a car? I'm sure you were terrified. Of course you were, you're controlling a thousand-pound death machine going 70 mph. Not just in drivers ed, but with your learners permit and probably your first couple months on the road. After years on the road, you now drive without thinking. Putting on lipstick, texting, changing your music, at this point you have so much confidence in your driving that you're willing to make it your secondary concern. That's the kind of tolerance you have to build to failure.

My first job out of college I spent half my day cold calling CEO's. I thought getting rejected from the prom was a horrifying experience, imagine getting told off by a coked-out executive. It was covid, a fresh college graduate working for a big firm and I had no idea what the fuck I was doing. To make matters worse I was living at my parents' house, it almost felt like I was cosplaying being a businessman on zoom. My job was to sell advice to c-suite executives. In no way at 22 years old was I qualified to have these conversations. With 6 weeks of training under my belt, I picked up the phone and dialed. My first 60 calls went right to voicemail (which was honestly a relief). Then at call 61 a man picked up, he was the CEO of a major distribution company in the Midwest. I did the classic young sales guy *"Hi X, this is Pat Broe with company x calling about.."* He stopped me right there. *"What are you selling me?"* he said assertively, my palms sweat, I was hoping we would work our way around the whole buying from me thing until he really liked me after a comfortable ten conversations. My voice cracked *"um, well, I'm calling because I noticed on your website.."* he stopped me again. *"What was your name, Matt? Please don't waste my time, what are you selling me?"* he said as his voice became angrier. *"Well you see, um I think you could improve your spend on..."* he stopped me a third time. *"Listen I get calls from salespeople all day, and none of you will just come out and say it. Stop wasting my time, and for god sakes sound like you actually believe what you are saying"* ***click***.

Now this was obviously mortifying. But I learned two valuable lessons, don't waste peoples time, and you better know what the fuck you're talking about. So I changed my strategy, I studied every business I needed to reach out down to what the CEO ate for lunch. I stayed up all night filling up pages with notes for weeks. Every time I made a call, my research gave me a goldmine of information about them, their problems and how I could help. When I called I got right to the point. I still had some work to do on not being nervous sounding, but that came with time and many more failures. Each call got easier, I was told 'no' thousands of times, but learned something in each interaction. It got easier every time and eventually rejection held no sting at all. In 6 months I was one of the top sellers in the company as a rookie, I smashed records and it gave my career a launchpad (I didn't do this by myself, my team was amazing, and our leader Jon Saenz is the best coach I've ever had. There is no such thing as a self-made man). The point being, rip the fucking band aid off for the things you want. You probably have no idea what you're doing, neither does anyone else so be the person that tries and learns.

Here is the final problem with failure, it threatens our ego. If you don't fail, you'll never know what's wrong with you and that feels safe. We all would like to think we know everything and will do anything to protect it. Simply letting yourself do something that might not work out is mortifying because the idea of being wrong is too painful. We are willing to forgo our dreams just because of the judgment we may feel if we fall short. When you let others take the power of chasing what you actually want away from you it leaves you helpless. Every time you say no to what you want because of how you may be judged you are letting other people control your life. Fuck them. It's your turn. Step up to the plate, and swing. Not for anyone else, but you. You may take a curveball to the nuts, but you'll have another chance. Learn the pitcher, and you will be smacking home runs before you know it. Tara Westover's book *Educated* covers this territory incredibly well. She grew up in a Mormon separatist cult, being that she was brilliant eventually she went off to college. Leaving the cult, she got exposed to the real world and the lies her father was feeding the family. She would go back home and try to help her family see the light, but their egos were too strong to risk making a change in their lives despite clear evidence they should. In discussing this Tara says:

"To admit uncertainty is to admit to weakness, to powerlessness, and to believe in yourself despite both. It is a frailty, but in this frailty there is a strength: the conviction to live in your own mind, and not in someone else's[80]."

Don't let your ego win, risk failure. You'll be better off for it.

Your Weakness May be a Superpower

You already have everything you need, but you are not perfect. Every piece of who you are is a part of a unique mix of possibilities literally only you can bring to the world. The skills you have are completely unique to you. We lack confidence because we don't think we have the right skill to be who we want to be or achieve what we want. The truth is, you have everything you need, you just might be using it wrong. And our perceived weaknesses are often our greatest strengths. Take for instance, those on the autism spectrum. Autistic people are often cast as unintelligent or strange due to the nature of the condition. Individuals with autism often face challenges in securing employment due to potential difficulties with skills like eye contact, communication, and other abilities typically valued in the workplace. That uniqueness is not a weakness, it's a superpower. People on the autism spectrum have a wide

---

[80] Westover, Tara. *Educated*. Windmill Books, 2018.

variety of characteristics (hence the spectrum) we would not associate with a neurotypical person. One of these behaviors include a tendency to hyper fixate. Keivan Stassun at NASA knew this all too well, with an autistic son at home he not only empathized with people on the spectrum, but where most people see a weakness he saw a strength. Keivan was working on data collected by the Kepler Space telescope. Kepler was launched into space to collect data to find other Earth-like planets. On its mission, Kepler collected data on 530,506 stars and 2,778 confirmed planets. That's a shitload of data to make sense of. To find patterns in that kind of data set he needed someone with a unique ability. That person was Dan Burger. Dan is on the autism spectrum, and Keivan sought him out for that very reason. His assignment was to help the team find patterns in the wide data set. Dan's autism did not make it tougher to find these patterns, it made him the perfect man for the job. That hyper fixation and unique view of the world gave Dan a perspective on the data none of his peers even dreamed of. With that Dan created an interactive software program named Filtergraph, enabling NASA to visualize vast datasets from the Kepler Telescope. This tool allows them to manipulate the data in various ways, helping them identify the patterns they seek. With Dan's tool in hand, he transformed the data into a visualization that the team could play with and find patterns in. Thanks to Dan's work, NASA has discovered a technique for determining the size and age of stars by analyzing their flickering intensity in telescope images. This discovery represents a significant milestone in advancing our scientific comprehension of space dynamics. *"I think my greatest skill is I see things differently from other people"* says Dan[81]. We should be thankful he doesn't. Keiven refused to see autistic people as less than but rather born with superpowers the rest of us can't see unless we let them show us.

---

[81] Morey, Eliabeth. "Man with Autism Invents Interactive Software to Help NASA Analyze Complex Data." *The Autism Cite*, https://blog.theautismsite.greatergood.com/nasa-software/.

That lives within all of us, but the only way to find it is persevering through discomfort. Struggle unlocks superpowers in you that you don't know yet exist. Frankly, we often misjudge ourselves and what is a "weakness" can be our best tool. We have attributes and characteristics and how we use them in the context of our lives makes them valuable or detrimental. No one sees the world like you. Isn't that fucking cool? So how do we take the parts that are perceived as weaknesses and use them to our advantage? We do tough shit.

Dan didn't sit around letting the world judge him for his autism, he found a way to use it for his advantage. Yes his unique set of skills gave him an advantage, but most importantly he worked really damn hard. He didn't sit in front of his computer and like a wizard the software program appeared. He put in the work. Whatever it is you are not confident about, the only true way to know how to use it is to put in the work. Whatever your dream is, get up and go chase it. What work are weaknesses will turn out to be strengths, exposing them takes dedication to a chosen craft. I'm sure Dan didn't always think of his autism as a blessing, it was only through work that he got the confidence to find the value of it. I don't just mean this in a capitalistic sense either. Work really hard on whatever you value, your relationship, hobby, or dream. Throw yourself fully at something and you'll find your superpower. Elbow grease is our mind's best medicine.

Be honest with yourself

Who are you? Not the nouns you use to describe your career or year in school. The actual you. Your characteristics, good and bad. What makes you, you? We lie to ourselves often. It comes naturally. However, taking a moment to level set and understand where you currently are will help you put your energy into things that will actually help you become The Real Confident You. Often we will dump our energy into what we are already good at. It's more comfortable there. But to actually grow and change you have to look at the ugly. Also, we do a pretty poor job of giving ourselves credit for what we do well. There is so much you could be taking confidence in that you don't. Not to mention if you know you have it, you'll use it more. *If ya got it, flaunt it, hun.*

Below is a great method to take an accurate assessment of yourself at this very moment. Any business student has done a SWOT analysis before. A SWOT analysis is typically done by a business to get a good understanding of their current place in the market, what they need to be concerned about from their competition and where they can improve against their goals. Modifying this, we can use it to take stock in where we sit today and what we can do to improve.

Self SWOT Analysis

First let's define some terms. You will be evaluating yourself across four categories. Strengths, weaknesses, opportunities, and threats. Defined as:

Strengths: These are internal factors that give us an advantage.

Now ask yourself:

- What are my inherent strengths?

- What unique advantages do I possess?

- How would my boss, teacher or friends describe my strong points? (If you don't know, ask them!)

- What accomplishments, whether in education or skills, distinguish me from my peers?

- What connections or resources do I have that can support me?

Weaknesses: These are internal factors that place us at a disadvantage compared to others.

Now ask yourself:

- What negative habits or traits do I possess?

- In which areas do I lag behind my peers in terms of education, training, or skills?

- Which skills do I aspire to enhance?

- What tasks do I avoid due to a lack of confidence?

- Reflecting on a work-related mistake, what actions did I take?

Opportunities: These are external factors that you could capitalize on to achieve your goals.

Now ask yourself:

- What negative habits or traits do I possess?

- Are there areas where I lack compared to my peers in terms of education, training, or skills?

- Which skills do I aim to enhance?

- What tasks do I shy away from due to a lack of confidence?

- Reflecting on a work-related mistake, what actions did I take?

Threats: These are external factors that could potentially harm you or your goals.

Now ask yourself:

- What is the current status of my industry or goals? Is it experiencing growth?

- Which new technologies could assist me in accomplishing my objectives?

- How can my network aid me in progressing?

- What additional skills can I develop to enhance my value?

- Are there strategic maneuvers, such as a career change or lateral transition, which could expedite my progress toward my goals?

- What habits or social circles do I have that may take away from my goal?

Take out your notes app/piece of paper and list the characteristics of yourself that you would consider in each category.

In this example Darius is thirty-two and struggling with his career. His lack of career progress is giving him large amounts of anxiety, but he doesn't know how to fix it.

Darius's SWOT Analysis	
Strengths:	**Weaknesses:**
Creative Mindset, enabling me to devise unique and efficient solutions.	Procrastination, struggle with maintaining the necessary discipline to finish
Thrives under pressure and excels in fast-paced environments.	Poor time management - frequently late
Highly organized and pays close attention to detail.	Confrontational - easily angered by coworkers and friends and have a hard time expressing it
Friendly and Approachable.	Reserved - too shy to voice thoughts
Resourceful	Anxious public speaking
Insightful, asks questions leading to valuable and informative responses while demonstrating genuine interest in others' perspectives.	Hard time expressing opinions when uncomfortable

Opportunities:	Threats:
At present, our company is failing to tap into a crucial market segment. I believe drafting a proposal outlining strategies to target this market could greatly impress my boss.	As technology progresses, my role might demand further education or specialized skills.
Leveraging technological advancements such as ChatGPT and other AI tools could significantly enhance my productivity.	I tend to finish projects at a slower pace compared to my peers.
Seeking guidance from one of my mentors for career advice or a potential recommendation for the position I am pursuing is a proactive step I could take.	My negative habits, such as procrastination and tardiness, could lead recruiters and managers to perceive me as unreliable.
Utilizing my off hours to enroll in an online course and expand my skill set would be beneficial.	The rise of AI programs poses a risk of making my current job obsolete, prompting me to consider preparing for a potential career transition.
Collaborating with a career coach to refine my interviewing skills prior to applying for a new position could improve my chances of success.	In my rapidly expanding industry, there is a constant influx of new college graduates entering the workforce, intensifying the competition I face.

Now Darius knows where he can focus his time and improve his position. Instead of just worrying, he knows what he can work on. His anxiety is replaced with a plan.

Seeking discomfort:

I've been dancing around this the whole chapter. You're probably too comfortable. Doing hard things is good for you and you're avoiding it. To be resilient you have to practice it, constantly. Confidence comes from challenging yourself and realizing you are capable of much more than you ever dreamed. Your brain produces four main chemicals that make you happy or feel positive emotions: Dopamine, Oxytocin, Serotonin, and Endorphins. Modernity is built on using these chemicals to addict you to quick fixes. Like hits of a drug TikTok IV drips little hits of dopamine as you scroll. Like any good drug, it gives you just enough to come back for more. It's not just social media, food, porn, alcohol you name it. These things we take comfort in give us a semblance of happiness, but it's fleeting. Nothing artificial is as good as the real thing. True happiness is the opposite of a quick fix.

What's the replacement? Doing things that aren't instantly comfortable. Seeking discomfort makes us happier. I know it seems paradoxical, but it's true. Unlike the instant happiness of your Frappuccino at Starbucks, doing something really challenging creates a happiness that's not fleeting. Partially because the fruits of labor just tend to last longer, but also our reward mechanisms are built that way. Here is the paradox - our brains continually assess the costs and benefits of our decisions and actions. During periods of intense work, the anterior cingulate cortex, situated near the front of the brain, monitors our exertion, with its neural activity linked to the perceived discomfort of the effort. These signals of effort assist our brain in determining whether it's worthwhile to persist or opt for an alternative course of action[82]. This mechanism needs

---

[82] Sima, Richard. "How to train your brain to enjoy doing hard things - The Washington Post." *Washington Post*, 29 September 2022,

training. It won't know the hard thing gives you a reward unless you constantly do it. Additionally, for things truly meaningful the reward will not be instantaneous. This is why first-time gym goers struggle horribly to find the motivation, but after years people say "they can't live without the gym". The people who constantly go to the gym over time have felt the rewards enough times that their brain no longer perceives the gym as a risk. Subsequently the long-term gym goer gets the benefits of consistent gym going like mood stabilization, and better sense of wellbeing. The gym goer also has the benefit of feeling accomplished, not only do they have the increased endorphins after a workout, but a sense of pride in the progress they have made.

While our brain tries to fight us doing uncomfortable things because it doesn't know the risks, it rewards us significantly when we actually do them. Neuroimaging studies indicate that the ventral striatum, a brain region crucial for processing rewarding outcomes, exhibits greater activation when we accomplish tasks through higher effort compared to lower effort[83]. So if you want to experience deep rewarding happiness, you have to do something hard.

I get that working out is a crutch I lean on because I am a meathead. But it doesn't apply just to David Goggins kind of hard. These kinds of reward systems work best when we are actually putting in our full effort to anything. People generally do enough to get by. They go to work but do the bare minimum, go to school but do just enough to get to the next grade etc. We trade momentary comfort for long term happiness every

---

https://www.washingtonpost.com/wellness/2022/09/29/train-brain-for-hard-things/. Accessed 30 March 2024

[83] Sima, Richard. "How to train your brain to enjoy doing hard things - The Washington Post." *Washington Post*, 29 September 2022, https://www.washingtonpost.com/wellness/2022/09/29/train-brain-for-hard-things/. Accessed 30 March 2024

time we don't give our best effort. You have to learn to cut that kind of thinking out if you want to be The Real Confident You. Just good enough may be fine for your boss, but it's not ok for someone seeking a fulfilling life. To be fulfilled you need to do something inherently fulfilling. There is nothing that is fulfilling that doesn't require your full effort. Every time you think "it's too hard", "I deserve a break", "I'll do it tomorrow", "this is so unfair" you are missing the opportunity to change your life forever. Happy aren't the people who "don't give a shit" they are the people inherently give a shit. Something that is instantly gratifying like TikTok is much easier to access but not only does the little happiness you get from it quickly wash away, it leaves you with less happiness than you started with. Whereas something that is much harder to access (for instance being the top of your class at cosmetology school) gives you large amounts of happiness and it lasts a lifetime. Think about the happiest moments in your life. Were they easy to get to? You know why men are obsessed with their high school athletic careers decades later? Because it was the last time they put their full effort into something and saw the rewards. That kind of work gives you positive memories that bring you happiness for a lifetime. Imagine if you built your entire life around creating those kinds of memories?

Being someone who does things the hard way isn't normal. This isn't normal. But normalness isn't making people happy, normality is making all of us unhappy. So why the fuck would you do what's normal. Starting today you are going to stop using normality as the measuring stick. As a matter of fact, you are going to stop measuring yourself by others in general. No one is going to change your world but you. People who let you make excuses for yourself aren't doing you any favors. And letting other people bring you down with their own excuses is even worse. Here is the new and only way you are going to measure yourself. Did I do my

<u>best?</u> If you didn't that's ok. But it starts tomorrow, the day after that and every day from here on out. Start stacking days of giving it your best behind you and see your life transform. Your best won't be the same every day. Shit happens.

Take out a piece of paper and write this:

My name is ____ and I love doing hard shit. No matter what, I give life my best effort. My happiness is not subject to the excuses that everyone else makes. More importantly I am done making excuses for myself, because goddamnit I am ____ and I am capable of anything. I want you to put that somewhere you can see it. Your bathroom mirror, laptop, make it the lockscreen on your phone. Until you embrace that to grow you are going to have to put your best effort forward, then you have no shot at becoming <u>The Real Confident You.</u>

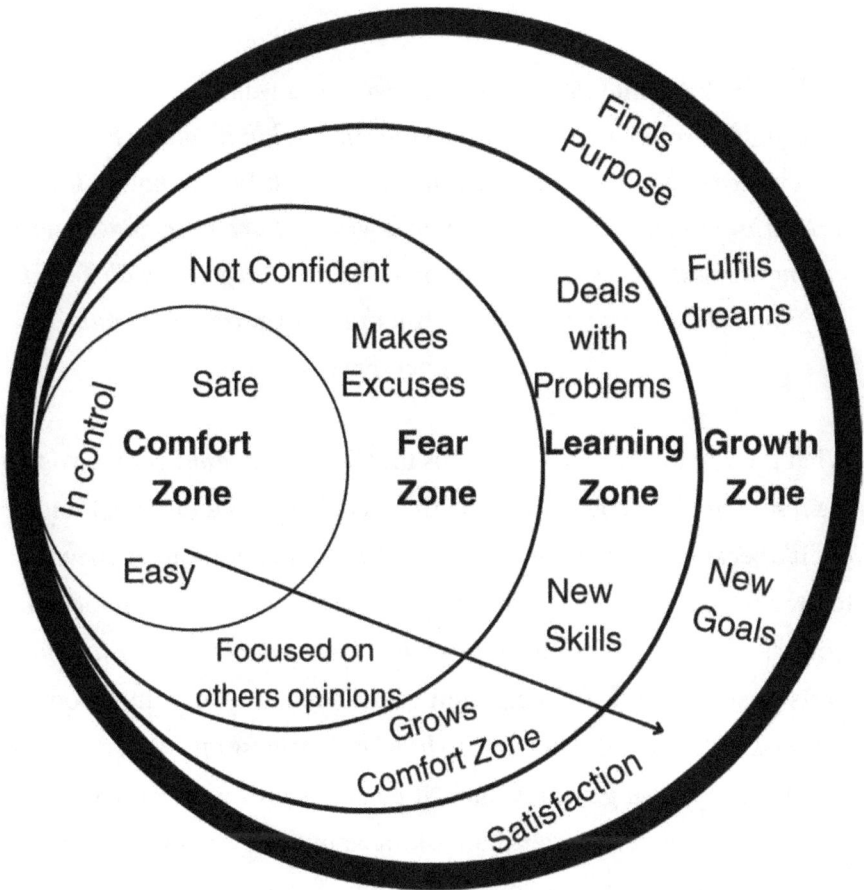

Chapter 8:

What's Your Goal?

"Oscar Wilde said that if you know what you want to be, then you inevitably become it - that is your punishment, but if you never know, then you can be anything. There is a truth to that. We are not nouns, we are verbs. I am not a thing - an actor, a writer - I am a person who does things - I write, I act - and I never know what I am going to do next. I think you can be imprisoned if you think of yourself as a noun."
~ **Stephen Fry**

What are you looking for out of this life? The *"what am I going to do for the rest of my life"* question is one that people spend a lifetime hung up on. It's because it's the wrong question. Work is important, I believe that to my core. But it isn't who you are. As a culture we are insistent on using work as the way to introduce ourselves. *"What do you do for a living?"* starts nearly every first interaction as an adult. If you're in school it's replaced with *"what do you want to be when you grow up?"* It makes sense For starters people generally suck at conversations with strangers, and you will get a better answer than asking about the weather. Secondly it reveals a lot about a person pretty instantly. Based on a person's job you can make safe assumptions on their social class, educational background, interests, and general aptitude. In my sales career we would call this a "qualifying question", the response you get will typically tell enough about a person's situation to grab details if you want to move forward or that the conversation is not worth your time. For instance, a kindergarten teacher and an escort probably know that they don't have much in common and can end the conversation pretty quickly. But if two people are in a similar place in life, they know they have opened many conversation branches to climb. While it's convenient for conversation, this focus on career does trap people (especially young) into self-actualizing through their job. Remember we no longer measure ourselves on the judgment of others but it's hard not to live a life that's career dependent when every Thanksgiving your drunk uncle asks what you are going to do with your life. But that is not a story, it is not a person. Work is just a mechanism to get you where you want to be. And it's one of many mechanisms, the rest of which we don't give enough attention to in our identity. If what you truly want is some career goal, great! I am one of those people and there is nothing wrong with that. But there are many more aspects of life to build around than just your 9-5. We shouldn't feel inadequacies about ourselves if our career doesn't dazzle but the portions of our life we care about more deeply are what gets our attention. When we think our career is going to fulfill all of our deepest desires it puts undue pressure on it to realize that. Subsequently any job that isn't our Barbie Dreamhouse imagination's level of fulfilling feels lackluster.

Take for instance a mother who wants to take a step back from her career because she is getting more fulfillment at home with her child. Should she feel shamed for not wanting to chase her career? Fuck no she shouldn't, she should feel like the most badass mom on Earth. She is doing the most important thing a human should do (we really need to fix our maternity leave laws). Now should she be held back in her career if that is the pursuit she still wants, absolutely not. But if she chooses motherhood over working in an office then dammit we should commend that (or a father in the same scenario). Now don't think I am making an excuse for you to be a lazy fuck. You still have responsibilities that I promise you will be much more fulfilled in obliging than not. Work is important, but I warn you not to overvalue it as you set the goals for becoming <u>The Real Confident You.</u> I wanted to preface with this before our goal setting conversation because this could take a very "entrepreneurship bro" tone. That is not what I am intending. However, thinking you will get fulfillment without setting real goals and the subsequent plan to achieve them is like throwing a penny in a fountain. An objective without a goal is not an objective, it's a wish at best. More importantly, a goal without a plan is a dream. For us to realize <u>The Real Confident You</u> we have to set goals around the things we actually want, not just superficial things we can say about ourselves at a bar. From there we can build a plan to actually achieve it. In this chapter you will learn how to properly set goals and build plans around them. This way you can finally be programmatic about living a better life. Having something to measure your progress against is not only great for your self-esteem, it's the only way to know you are getting better.

Most of us suck at goal setting. When we set poor goals, we have poor execution. Saying "I want to be better at tennis" isn't a goal, it's a wish. So what is a proper goal?

SMART Goals Revisited:

We talked about this briefly in chapter 4, but let's take a deeper dive. I imagine at some point in middle or high school you came across SMART goals if you are under 30. You probably haven't used them once since. The problem with most goal setting is there is no structure. There is no accountability and nothing you can build an actual plan around. If the President of the United States came on TV and said, *"we are going to reduce carbon emissions"*. Immediately reporters would ask *"by how much"*, *"by when"*, *"how are you going to do it"*, *"are you able to do it?"*.

As they should, just saying you're going to reduce something isn't exactly a goal for a nation. That kind of scrutiny is expected to understand how the job is going to get done. So why aren't you applying the same level of scrutiny to yourself? Also, in the process of building a goal you should get an idea of the steps you need to take to achieve it.

SMART goals are crucial because they provide clarity and focus, ensuring that individuals understand precisely what needs to be accomplished and can avoid distractions. They are measurable, allowing progress to be tracked objectively and adjustments to be made if necessary. By encouraging realistic and achievable objectives, SMART goals help individuals set targets that are within reach and promote a sense of motivation. The time-bound aspect of SMART goals creates a sense of urgency, motivating individuals to work consistently towards achieving their goals within a specified timeframe. Overall, SMART goals promote effective goal-setting practices that lead to increased productivity, motivation, and success in achieving desired outcomes. Let's revisit the SMART goal framework this time with a little more detail:

Specific: Goals should be clear and specific, focusing on a particular area for improvement or accomplishment. For example, "Improve communication skills" is specific, while "Be better at everything" is too vague.

Questions to address:

- What is my objective?

- Why does this goal matter?

- Who is participating?

- Where is this taking place?

- What resources or constraints are involved?

Measurable: Goals should be quantifiable so that progress can be tracked and evaluated. For instance, "Read 20 pages of a book each day" is measurable, whereas "Read more" is not specific enough to measure progress.

Questions to address:

- What is the quantity?

- How many are involved?

- How will I recognize when it's achieved?

Achievable: Goals should be realistic and attainable within the given timeframe and resources available. Setting goals that are too ambitious or beyond your current capabilities can lead to frustration and lack of motivation.

Questions to address:

- What are the steps to achieve this goal?

- How feasible is the goal considering other constraints?

Relevant: Goals should be relevant to your overall objectives and priorities. They should align with your values, aspirations, and long-term plans. For example, if your long-term goal is to become a software engineer, learning coding languages would be relevant.

Questions to address:

- Is this worthwhile?

- Is now the appropriate time?

- Does this align with our other initiatives/requirements?

- Am I a suitable individual to achieve this goal?

Time Bound: Goals should have a deadline or timeframe for completion. This helps create a sense of urgency and accountability. For instance, "Lose 10 pounds in two months" is time-bound, while "Lose weight" lacks a specific timeframe.

Questions to address:

- At what time?

- What actions can I take in six months?

- What tasks can I accomplish in six weeks?

- What steps can I take today?

Now let's take a good SMART goal and break it down by its parts.

- **Jorgens Mindfulness Goal:** My goal is to reduce stress and improve mental health through consistent mindfulness practices. I will achieve this by meditating for 10 minutes every morning and evening by March 30th (3 months from now). I'll start with 5-minute sessions and work towards 10 minutes February 30th. This goal is relevant to me as mindfulness practices are known to reduce stress and improve mental health. I aim to establish this routine within three months, ensuring I meditate for 10 minutes twice a day every day.

Specific:

- *"through consistent mindfulness practices"* Jorgen is not only accounting for his intention, but what he will do to accomplish this.

Measurable:

- "meditating for 10 minutes every morning and evening" is a specific success metric to hold himself to.

Achievable:

- *"5-minute sessions and work towards 10 minutes February 30th"* by setting realistic benchmarks and progressions Jorgen keeps the goal reasonable and something he can achieve.

Relevant:

- "mindfulness practices are known to reduce stress and improve mental health"/ "mindfulness practices are known to reduce stress and improve mental health" Jorgen both says why the goal is important to him and how meditation is relevant to that goal

Time Bound:

- *"by March 30th (3 months from now)"*/ "I aim to establish this routine within three months, ensuring I meditate for 10 minutes twice a day every day." He states the exact time structure he is holding himself accountable to.

Based on Jorgen's goal it is much easier to make a plan to succeed. In fact the plan is within the goal. Something more expansive like a large career or personal aspiration will take a more thought out plan, but a SMART goal gives that plan a great North Star to fall back on.

What Motivates Us?

Do you like conspiracy theories? Be honest we all kinda do. Some of them are fun! Who doesn't want to believe the government has a secret program where they're hiding all the aliens. They get pretty kooky but if you just use them as a thought experiment there is typically no harm in a little YouTube rabbit hole every once and awhile. One group of conspiracy theorists have done great damage too is the organization that invented the term, the CIA. I mention this because they tend to get a bad rap (partially because of their own doing, have you ever read about MK Ultra?). However there is no doubting their effectiveness, especially when it comes to evaluating and recruiting spies. Keeping America safe is tough business and a little espionage is part of the game. To collect the information that keeps us safe CIA operatives undergo training to enlist individuals from foreign countries as spies for the United States. To convince anyone to do your bidding, you need to understand their motivations. The CIA uses the MICE framework to understand a potential spy's motivations. It's both a euphemism for a rat (see Goodfellas) and an acronym for Money, Ideology, Coercion, and Ego[84]. These four things get to the core of what humans are motivated by. Our motivations drive and direct us to take action, pursue goals, and seek satisfaction. The CIA understands that if you can fulfill someone's motivations, you can get them to do actions (even if it makes them a traitor). The CIA defines the MICE motivations as:

---

[84] Morton, Robert. ""MICE"- the 4 pillars of CIA spy recruitment | by Robert Morton | Medium." *Robert Morton*, 8 January 2022, https://spyauthor.medium.com/mice-the-4-pillars-of-cia-spy-recruitment-61d3f5cf9d3c. Accessed 1 April 2024.

Money	Ideology
Money serves as a powerful motivator for individuals due to its ability to provide security, comfort, and opportunities for personal and professional growth. The security that comes with financial stability allows us to meet our basic needs and reduces stress associated with survival. Moreover, money enables us to enjoy a comfortable lifestyle, affording us conveniences and experiences that enhance our well-being. It also plays a role in status and recognition, serving as a symbol of success and providing a sense of accomplishment and esteem.	Individuals are often motivated by ideology due to its power to provide a sense of belonging, purpose, and direction in life. Ideologies, whether political, religious, or philosophical, offer a framework of beliefs, values, and principles that guide individuals' thoughts, actions, and decisions. Belonging to an ideology can create a sense of community and connection with like-minded individuals, fostering a supportive network and camaraderie. Moreover, ideologies often serve as sources of inspiration and motivation, fueling individuals' efforts to work towards a shared vision or goal. Additionally, ideologies can drive individuals to advocate for change, pursue social justice, or strive for a better world according to their ideological convictions.

Coercion	Ego
Coercion can serve as a motivator through fear of consequences, desire for rewards, and social pressure. Fear-based motivation arises when individuals comply to avoid punishment or loss, while the promise of rewards incentivizes compliance. Social coercion, driven by social norms and expectations, can also push individuals to conform to avoid social repercussions. However, while coercion can produce short-term compliance, it often leads to negative consequences such as resentment and lack of intrinsic motivation, highlighting the importance of fostering intrinsic motivation based on personal values and interests for sustainable and fulfilling outcomes.	We are motivated by ego due to its role in shaping our self-image, self-worth, and social status. Ego-driven motivation stems from a desire for validation, recognition, and superiority. Individuals seek to enhance their self-esteem and self-confidence by achieving success, receiving praise, and gaining admiration from others. Ego can drive competitive behavior, ambition, and a desire to stand out or excel in various aspects of life, such as career achievements, academic accomplishments, or social status.

Now what the CIA won't tell you is these motivators won't necessarily bring you to a fulfilling life. Any motivation that could lead you down the road of becoming a traitor to your own people you should take a pause in. In fact, the CIA teaches its own agents how NOT to be influenced by these kinds of motivators. They even avoid agents who could fall prey to them, for instance they don't hire agents in poor financial situations because they may be likely to flip if offered money[85]. When looking for a carrot to dangle for motivation, MICE serves as a warning for motivations that can make your life a zero-sum game.

While some motivations can lead us down undesired paths, motivation is important. Strong motivation enables us to excel, while its absence can lead to stagnation. Heightened motivation gives our lives enhanced involvement, improved contentment, flourishing interpersonal connections, and thriving institutions. However, it's often hard to find. Knowing which carrots to dangle in front of us in a healthy and productive way is essential to becoming The Real Confident You. When we set goals, we need a fire under us to do the actions. In achieving any goal there will be tradeoffs. Greta Gerwig (director of hit movies like *Barbie*) said in an interview *"When you're on set, and that clock is going, every second you spend doing something is a second you spend not doing something else. That's true of all of life"*[86]. It may seem simple, but in any goal you will have to sacrifice something in order to achieve something else. When we align our goals with our self-actualizing motivations it makes that trade-off significantly easier. The motivations laid out by The

---

[85] D'Agati, Caroline. "Want to Fight Insider Threats? Just Look for the MICE." *Security Clearance News & Career Advice*, 2 August 2019, https://news.clearancejobs.com/2019/08/02/want-to-fight-insider-threats-just-look-for-the-mice/. Accessed 1 April 2024.

[86] The Hollywood Reporter. "Directors Roundtable: Todd Phillips, Martin Scorsese, Greta Gerwig, Noah Baumbach | Close Up." *YouTube*, 6 January 2020, https://www.youtube.com/watch?v=4iLtjMwkOlg. Accessed 1 April 2024.

CIA are all <u>extrinsic motivations</u> which entails participating in an activity with the expectation of receiving a concrete reward or avoiding negative consequences[87]. For example, *"I do all my homework because my mom said I can play Fortnite on Saturday if I do"*. This also entails using others' opinions to motivate us, like getting in shape for the sole reason of getting compliments. When we think of motivating factors this is often what we think of, doing a task for the reward at the end. While this is helpful in the short term, it often does not lead to consistency or fulfillment.

Instead, when looking for motivation that leads to long-term fulfilling success we should look to <u>intrinsic motivation</u>. Intrinsic motivation is when we do something because we find it fascinating and fulfilling. We're drawn to these activities because they make us feel good. Studies tell us that when we're intrinsically motivated, we stick with things longer, feel better mentally, and perform better[88]. Our motivation typically falls into a spectrum of extrinsic to intrinsic. Our motivations are not binary. There are often multiple streams of influence coming on a particular motivation. For instance, you may be motivated to get a promotion at work because it will give you more rewarding work <u>and</u> it will impress your friends. See the spectrum evidenced below:

---

[87] Deci, Edward L., and Richard R. Ryan. "Self-determination theory: A macrotheory of human motivation, development, and health." *APA PsycNet*, 2008, https://psycnet.apa.org/record/2008-10897-002. Accessed 1 April 2024.

[88] Souders, Beata, and Maike Neuhaus. "The Vital Importance and Benefits of Motivation." *Positive Psychology*, 5 November 2019, https://positivepsychology.com/benefits-motivation/#important. Accessed 1 April 2024.

Spectrum of Self Determination

Non-self Determined ◄- -► Self Determined

Not Motivated	Extrinsic Motivation		Intrinsic Motivation
No Control	Externally Motivated	Rewards	High Pleasure
Incompetence	Ego Involvement	Punishment	Satisfaction
No Choice	Obidience	Pride/guilt	Interest
No Intention	External Focus	Compliance	Fun
			Engagement

Ryan, R. M. & Deci, E. L. (2017). Self-determination theory: Basic psychological needs in motivation, development, and wellness. The Guilford Press. https://doi.org/10.1521/978.14625/28806

Being aware of where your motivations fall on the spectrum can help you push yourself in the direction of intrinsic motivation. You should be achieving your goal because the action itself brings enhancement to your life, not for rewards, punishments, or the praise of others. You should be looking to enhance your life, not enhance how people see you. So when looking for motivation, tie your action to something that is fulfilling. This isn't to say doing things for other people's benefit isn't a good motivation. That is much different than doing it for their praise. For instance, if you are up late studying you can think of the reward of a good grade on that the test you are studying for will allow you to do work that you love. If you focus on the fulfilling part and not the grade you will be more likely to follow through. Also, you will enjoy the work itself more. In short, focus on what parts of your goal make <u>you happy</u>. Focusing on rewards or other people's attention will leave you feeling shallow and less likely to actually follow through. Most importantly you need to find motivation in enjoying the action you are taking on, not just the reward. Find joy in climbing the mountain, not just the peak.

Finally, it's good to keep our motivations tidy. We get in our own way a lot, and often not finding motivation is just a symptom of being overwhelmed. We want to do something but are paralyzed by how much. To keep yourself from getting overwhelmed, make sure your goals align with this checklist.

1. **Autonomy** - To really own what you're doing, find ways to make it your own. For instance, if you're not a fan of running but want to get more active, think about other fun ways to exercise, like cycling or dancing.

2. **Competence** - Keep things challenging but doable. If it's too easy or too hard, you'll lose interest.

3. **Relatedness**- Feeling connected is important. Try doing your activity with a buddy or joining a group. You can also help others get into it too, like sharing your tips and experiences.

4. **Values Alignment** - Make sure what you're doing lines up with what matters to you. And if it doesn't directly, make a case for it. For instance, maybe your job isn't fulfilling, but family is important to you. Make your work about the money that will go to them.

5. **Removing Roadblocks**- Sometimes, stuff gets in the way of our motivation, like too many goals at once or not getting enough rest. Identify what's holding you back and clear those obstacles.

But I still haven't found what I'm looking for:

"Ok great Pat, I know how to set a goal now, and how to get motivated, I still don't know what I want". I can't answer this question for you. However, if you integrate what we have talked about this far the answer will come. My suggestion to you is merely that, a suggestion. This is my direct lived experience talking here. Needless to say the suicidal 16-year-old version of me was lost on the answers of what I wanted. However, I just picked a direction and sprinted. Sometimes we need to get out of our analysis paralysis and just do it. I learned a lot about myself and what fulfilled my life. I got metaphorically punched in the face a lot (non-metaphorically too). Only from there could I actually see what I truly wanted. Also because I put in the effort, doors opened much easier. Don't waste your time looking for the perfect thing to emerge. Despite the studies, YouTube gurus, BuzzFeed quizzes and the entire industry built on finding the perfect career/spouse/hobby etc. that will fit your life, only you can really figure that out.

My suggestion is whatever you are doing right now in your career or otherwise, dedicate your all to it. Passively participating in life bears no answers. When you give it your all you quickly find out what you like or don't like. Try hard at being a good friend, and the responses back will quickly tell you what kind of friends you want in your life. Give your job your all, the parts of your job that you like will either keep you around or give you something to look for in your next job. Be the best romantic partner you can, your partner will show you what you're looking for. Take accountability in your life and it will pay dividends. Try hard, and yes people will judge you. Those people just wish they could be you. Opportunities don't show up for something standing still. Don't wait for the perfect opportunity to set a goal, build goals around what you have so you get a perfect opportunity.

Congratulations on Completing Step 2

2/3rds of the way there. Can you believe it? We have come so far in this time. To reassess, in part one we learned about the inputs, how the modern world is causing our mental health problems. When your world is out of whack, start there. Once you've fixed your inputs, then it's time to do the work. The work is fixing the damage you've accrued over time. Now it's time for the grand finale. <u>The Real Confident You.</u> Think of part one as learning where you are missing soil, part two as filling in the dirt. Now in part three it's time to plant the tree.

Oh and one more thing, did you remember to practice your breathing?

Part 3:
The Real Confident You

Chapter 9:

Confidence Through Mastery

———— ·· ❧ ❧ ·· ————

"Although the butterfly and the caterpillar are completely different, they are one in the same" ~ **Kendrick Lamar**

Imagine it's 1606 and you are walking around Japan. In this time machine, you want to see a Samurai. You've read so much about these warlords that you want to see it for yourself. You find out the best Samurai master in all of Japan is in your town. His name is Miyamoto Musashi, and you hear he is the best dueler of all time. So you track him down for a conversation. You find out where he is, and you are shocked at the sight you see. The most feared man in all of Japan is … painting? He isn't just painting, he is surrounded by nothing that would resemble an article of war. Sculptures, writings, carvings, and home improvement projects surround Musashi and all of his own doing[89]. His house resembles Leonardo Di Vinci's more than Alexander the Greats'. What you would soon find is this is all part of Musashi's success.

Mastery is a skill of its own. Miyamoto Musashi certainly thought so. There is a unique skill in understanding how to become great at something. So Miyamoto believed developing that skill by doing crafts like painting was much safer than practicing the skill of mastery across from another man with a sword. *"Once you understand the way broadly,*

---

[89] Kiyonaga, Torii. "The Action-Packed Life Of Japan's Greatest Duelist, Miyamoto Musashi." *The Historian's Hut*, 18 May 2017, https://thehistorianshut.com/2017/05/18/the-action-packed-life-of-japans-greatest-duelist-miyamoto-musashi/#google_vignette. Accessed 1 April 2024.

you can see it in all things" Musashi said in his most famous work, *The Book of the Five Rings*[90]. How would you know how to do something truly challenging if you've never done anything challenging before? Also, the confidence achieved through the process of mastery gives you the knowledge you can do it again.

Learning how you specifically handle hard tasks teaches us the most about our character. That knowledge rids self-doubt. When we discussed "The Self-esteem" movement, we talked about how self-esteem that isn't anchored to any real skill is easily lost if real at all. If you think confidence comes from thin air or you are born with it then you don't know how to build it. Confidence is not inherited, it is built. Musashi knew this inherently. If you want to be the best version of you then you have to have something to be confident about. Beauty fades, but a skill in life will always give you something to be confident of. We all have the ability to be great. Hence you are much surer of yourself when you have seen the greatness inside you in action. Truly dedicating yourself to something you're passionate about is the greatest confidence builder in the world because the process pays dividends.

In this chapter we will address how developing a skill will make you the most confident version of yourself. Or as some may say, <u>the real confident you.</u> Building your self-esteem starts with building something to anchor it to. Certainly, we are only born with the cards we are handed (which you should take pride in as well). To build confidence you have to actually play your cards, not stand and watch the game. Gaining confidence is an exercise in self-understanding. Confident people don't have less weaknesses, rather they are honest with themselves about them as well as their strengths. The best way to get to know yourself is an attempt at mastery. I don't mean you need to become a 17th century

---

[90] Musashi, Miyamoto. *Goodreads*. Translated by Victor Harris, Arcturus Publishing, 2018

swordsman. There are conventions for that kind of activity. What I am referring to is taking something in your life and giving it your 100% effort. Dreaming really big and dedicating your all to an important part of your life. Shooting for something you thought was impossible not for the reward at the end, but the rewards of the journey. Benjamin Hoff, the writer of *"The Tao of Pooh"* (a book about the lessons of Winnie the Pooh and their similarities to Taoism) said this about the joy built from the process:

> *"The Christmas presents once opened are Not So Much Fun as they were while we were in the process of examining, lifting, shaking, thinking about, and opening them. Three hundred sixty-five days later, we try again and find that the same thing has happened. Each time the goal is reached, it becomes Not So Much Fun, and we're off to reach the next one, then the next one, then the next.*
>
> *That doesn't mean that the goals we have don't count. They do, mostly because they cause us to go through the process and it's the process that makes us wise, happy, or whatever. If we do things in the wrong sort of way, it makes us miserable, angry, confused, and things like that. The goal has to be right for us, and it has to be beneficial, in order to ensure a beneficial process. But aside from that, it's really the process that's important."*

Complacency is built into modern society. Doing things the way everyone else does is celebrated. When we conform blindly, we restrict our potential and hurt our ability to embrace novel ideas and experiences. This can result in a sense of stagnancy and a loss of direction. You need to do specifically what no one else will do if you want to find true confidence. When you were a child, did you dream of having the most comfortable life possible or did you dream of chasing things you loved? You knew everything that makes a confident person as a 6-year-old, the world just told you otherwise. Let me be very clear, working an 8-hour day, coming home and plopping on the couch to binge TV will not make you happy. Once again, this could be misconstrued as a career advice pep talk, it's not. Our passions take many forms, but we trade them for momentary comforts. Want to change the world? Why not try to be the best humanitarian volunteer you can be in your free time, I'm sure your local food pantry needs help. The point being building self-confidence doesn't come passively. This is why getting uncomfortable is so important if you don't expose yourself to difficulty you will never know who you really are. Let's examine how you can use skill building to be <u>the real confident you</u>.

Start with what you love:

The easiest way to build confidence is to have a skill you are confident in. We aren't all going to be carpenters or great artists overnight, but I am sure there is something challenging to work on within arm's reach. You have a passion for something. It's time to lean in productively. What you are interested in is a great place to learn a skill. The difference between a skill and a hobby is that a skill can produce value for yourself and others. Watching baseball is a hobby, writing a blog about baseball is a skill. Tweeting about politics is a hobby, going to your city council meeting to fight for a cause is a skill. Many of us look at our passions passively. We look at our jobs for value, and our passions as escape. Your passion does not have to be your job to be happy but participating passively does not make us happy in the long term, only in the short.

For instance, lets you love video games. If you just play *God of War* at home, that's a hobby. It may be fun, but you are doing nothing but bringing momentary pleasure to yourself. However, starting a YouTube channel to talk about the lore of the *God of War* series, fantastic! Now you aren't only doing something you love, but it's creating value for yourself and potential viewers. Don't want to be a twitch streamer? Start a weekly meeting of other people who love the game. Virtually or in person create a space for people to bond in the things they love. Don't just go to the video game convention, find out how you can volunteer at the next event. Regardless, if you start with something you're passionate about, it's much easier to find skills to improve on that are actually beneficial. Would starting a hypothetical YouTube series about a video game be easy? Hell no! You'll have to learn about editing, lighting, copyright infringement, and 100 things I'm not thinking of. Your first 100 videos may have 13 views a piece. Not saying you're going to be Mr. Beast but if you stick to it long enough you will figure it out! That is the important part, the "figuring it out". When we give ourselves to something worth doing the "figuring it out" part is where we get our confidence.

Everybody's passion is weird to somebody. We often worry when we lean on what our friends or family may think. If anyone judges for you something you love, fuck them. If they aren't supporting you giving life your best, they aren't your friend. At 19 when I walked into our college radio station KQAL at the invitation of a young man named Tyler Jeffries and people thought I was fucking nuts. "Who does he think he is?" was the most common feeling I was met with. My only true loves in life were music, football, and conversation. I knew I wasn't going to be a radio host for a living, FM isn't exactly a growing industry. But the first time the microphone turned on it felt like a light went off in my brain. The things I normally just passively enjoyed were now not only active but creating value. My deep knowledge of dad rock wasn't just repulsing background noise for any girl I dated, but a tool to make my listeners have a happier ride to work. When I got the opportunity to be the radio voice of our football team, my knowledge of the spread offense wasn't a waste of time on the weekends, it helped our listeners understand what was happening on the field, often with their own sons playing. When I had to skip nights out because I wanted to save my voice for talking on a microphone for football, "friends" judged every step I made. The further I dedicated myself to this passion, people laughed at me for the more my confidence grew. Never did that shy kid think he could talk into a microphone for hours a day, and now people relied on me to do it! And guess what, I fucked up all the time! One time I forgot to turn on the automation machine when I left my shift and the station had dead air for 8 hours. Let me repeat, a radio station made no noise for an entire night. In every mistake I learned and grew, as a radio host sure, but as a person.

In 2018 I became the program director, the head honcho of the students at the station. Promptly upon taking the role the university cut the funding to our basketball broadcasts. I panicked. It was like being a president inheriting a war I didn't start. Doug Westerman, our General Manager (who is like a father to all the KQAL'rs) had a solution. *"Pat, go sell advertising"*. I had no fucking idea how to sell anything. But with Doug's encouragement, I went out to sell ads to keep our basketball broadcasts alive.

The first stop was the meeting I had set up with a local pizzeria. Palms sweaty I walked into the pizzeria on a freezing cold day. It was winter break, so the town had that eerie feeling of emptiness when students weren't around. I was wearing an ill-fitting suit I got from working at a Banana Republic in high school. I sat down at the empty restaurant with the owner and pitched him what the advertising would look like. The entire night before I practiced in the mirror what I would say until 3 am, but in the moment it flowed out like I was Jordan Belfort. When I got done with my pitch the owner looked at me and said, "I love it, where do I sign". I was a fucking natural (they actually never paid us, and their building burnt down over Covid, I'll let you be the judge of how that fire occurred, get the money upfront). Turns out, I loved sales, and I was damn good at it. That story got me an internship that would go on to change my life. The *"what do you want to do for a living"* question was answered for me completely unintentionally. never would have found the thing that makes me happiest in life if I didn't lean into something everybody thought was a waste of time.

Throwing yourself at something will pay endless dividends in life. This year I attended Tyler Jeffries' wedding. It was a reunion for all of us old KQAL'rs. Everything good in my life I can track back to giving it all to something that made no sense to anyone else. Not to mention when I did become successful at it, this weird life passion became a status symbol. It gave me a career, lifelong mentors, and friends, but most of all it gave me confidence. Taking a hobby and turning it into a skill transformed my existence in every possible way. Sure it is a stupid college radio station to most people, but to me it was my life. That's possible for you.

Here is the hard part, you have to do the work. None of this would be possible if I didn't show up every day for years. Showing up didn't just mean being there, it meant giving it my all. Never being "too cool" to do something, just doing it. I won't ask you for multiple years, but I am asking for one. Dedicate one year of your life to something that you are passionate about and watch your life flourish. The first couple months will be rough. People will judge you most when you are just trying to get something off the ground. Give it a year, one good year of showing up and improving 1% a day. Set a goal for a year from now and make a plan to get there. *"I don't have time"*, how much fucking tv do you watch. Look at your screen time, trust me you have the time. Take something you're passionate about, throw your everything at making it a skill. I promise the real confident you will be born.

The Critic Inside You:

Self-doubt is a real bitch. Hate to break it to you, you are influencing it. How we talk to ourselves affects our self-image. Research consistently indicates that self-criticism and negative self-talk are not only linked to stress and anxiety but also contribute to reduced self-confidence following setbacks or failures. Crucially, these studies demonstrate that self-criticism hinders goal achievement[91]. Neuroscience findings reveal that when engaging in self-criticism, our brains activate regions associated with emotions, self-referential memories, error monitoring, punishment, and behavioral inhibition[92]. Essentially, the self-critical mindset perceives setbacks as threats, triggering the brain's threat system. This mode also intensifies error monitoring, leading to self-punitive thoughts about perceived mistakes and fostering a hyper-focus on avoiding similar outcomes in the future.

First of all, it's completely normal to have negative self-talk. It's the default mode for all of us. The most confident person you know struggles with this. Whatever you can do to slow it down will be essential to finding the real confident you. Here are some great habits to get that negative voice to shut up as you build your skill.

---

[91] Raina, Shefai. "Four Brain Science Habits To Help Neutralize Negative Self-Talk." *Forbes.com*, 9 November 2017, https://www.forbes.com/sites/forbescoachescouncil/2021/05/06/four-brain-science-habits-to-help-neutralize-negative-self-talk/?sh=782be9dc4f3c. Accessed 3 April 2024.

[92] Raina, Shefai. "Four Brain Science Habits To Help Neutralize Negative Self-Talk." *Forbes.com*, 9 November 2017, https://www.forbes.com/sites/forbescoachescouncil/2021/05/06/four-brain-science-habits-to-help-neutralize-negative-self-talk/?sh=782be9dc4f3c. Accessed 3 April 2024.

My Head is an Asshole Free Zone

1. **See something, Say something:** When faced with a deeply ingrained mental habit like self-criticism and negative self-talk, a crucial step is to cultivate awareness and create distance from that narrative[93].

   a. Give a playful name to the self-criticism and negative self-talk, such as "Mr. Negative Self-Talk," to establish mental and emotional separation.

   b. Recognize the situations that trigger the negative self-talk pattern, such as rumination or self-criticism.

   c. Purposefully interrupt the self-talk and refrain from identifying with it. For instance, pause and acknowledge, "Here comes Mr. Negative Self-Talk again," affirming, "This isn't my core identity," and assert, "This isn't beneficial," then set that mental persona aside.

2. **Intentionally Own the Narrative:** Purposefully and intentionally say positive things to yourself. Force the creation of an internal culture of positivity within you.

   a. Set the intention of your breathwork practice to be changing your self-talk.

   b. Use reminders on your phone to remind intentionally say something positive

---

[93] Raina, Shefai. "Four Brain Science Habits To Help Neutralize Negative Self-Talk." *Forbes.com*, 9 November 2017, https://www.forbes.com/sites/forbescoachescouncil/2021/05/06/four-brain-science-habits-to-help-neutralize-negative-self-talk/?sh=782be9dc4f3c. Accessed 3 April 2024.

Creating positive self-talk is a constant battle, to win you have to stick to it. Repetition is key, you are trying to undo a lifetime of wiring, it will not happen overnight. Most importantly there will be times when you need to be critical of yourself. It's the only way to learn from a lesson. Just make sure that criticism is constructive. If your grandma wouldn't talk to you that way, don't say it to yourself.

Be a Goldfish:

Some of you may be wondering *"who is keeping AppleTv in business"*. That would be me. I'll come clean, I love Ted Lasso. For those who haven't seen the show, the premise is Ted Lasso is an American Football coach from Kansas who gets hired to run a premier league soccer team in England. When he is hired everyone thinks he's an idiot but in the process of coaching he teaches everyone life lessons with his wholesome midwestern wisdom winning over the team and fans. Completely corny but as a kid from the Midwest Ted reminds me of all the coaches I grew up with playing sports. One of the main comedic themes of the show is Ted's constant positivity and great sayings. When asked if he believes in ghosts Ted says *"I do. But more importantly, I believe they need to believe in themselves"*. My coaches all had great lines like Ted. For instance, my high school wrestling coach Joe Bavlnka used to say things like *"No sitting around this weekend eating bon bons."* It was 2015; not a single one of us knew what a bon bon was. He knew that, so he got his message across and got a laugh from the boys. Or his assistant and football coach Randy Ebright. He was one of those guys who seemed like a real hard-ass but was actually the nicest man you'll ever meet. He couldn't hear very well so his normal tone was more like a yell. Across a field you could hear things like, *"IT'S ALRIGHT, YOU CAN ALWAYS TRY AGAIN NEXT YEAR"* indicating that you were so dumb you would fail a grade and get to try again. He screamed as he stood there with a football taped to a hockey stick to replace the action of a ball snapping. I became a man from little notes of encouraging midwestern wisdom like Ted's. Even hard criticisms were funny in hindsight. I wasn't fast at all, so when a football coach suggested to me that I should line up closer to the quarterback to save everyone some time on a jet sweep he said, *"Pat you're a great kid, but you're so slow"*. That's both degrading and hilarious. The guy was so midwestern nice he felt the need to tell me I was a good person before breaking my heart. It wasn't just humor, quips from coaches ended up being great life lessons. Like Bryan Asbeck who said, *"don't be a scout team all-American"*, which means don't try hard just to ruin someone else's day, try hard when it actually matters. Midwesterners grow up surrounded by a bunch of tater tot casserole eating philosophers.

So needless to say Ted's Lasso gets to the root of who I am as a human being. In the first season of Ted Lasso, one of the players Sam Obisanya makes a mistake in practice and gets ridiculed by one of his teammates for it. Coach Lasso pulls Sam aside and asks him *"Sam, do you know what the happiest animal on Earth is?"*. Sam doesn't know so Ted answers *"It's a goldfish, it's got a 10 second memory, be a goldfish Sam"*. It's something I could hear our head football coach Steve Turkington saying after a tough play. Despite the comedy of it, there is sage wisdom there. In attempting anything challenging, you are going to run into trouble. When things are going well we like to fluff ourselves up, and when they go poorly we get too discouraged. "Being a goldfish" means we don't let either feeling last too long. In our successes and failures it is most important to just keep moving forward. Have a bad day at work? Move on. When we give our success or failure the power to change our moods then we are dependent on it for our confidence. Really, where your confidence should come from is your effort. You give a damn about something, be proud of that.

Chapter 10:

Burn The House that Ego Built

———— ··❀··❀·· ————

"It's not having what you want, It's wanting what you've got"
~ Sheryl Crow

You're saying goodbye to a person you have spent your whole life learning. That person is you. Scary right? It's why we don't address the things that cause us pain, because at least we understand it. That's no way to live a life my friend. To become <u>The Real Confident You</u>, there is a piece of you that you have to say goodbye to . And it's ok to be upset with that. Change strikes fear in all of us. It certainly does for me. Moving as constantly as I did I had a fear of loss that caused me to be over attached with objects and people. The thought of losing a dumb high school relationship was crippling just because I had no faith I would ever have a connection again. That may seem sad but there is a certain amount of ego in that. When we don't let people go even when we know it's best for them is the ultimate exercise in self-righteousness. It caused me to be overbearing, possessive, an objectifier, and jealous, all of which were my fault. Flaws that are all ego built. Nevertheless, letting go of that behavior was challenging because even when I knew those behaviors were wrong. It's a part of me I knew well, and changing meant accepting fault and learning a whole new way to be. Our ego driven flaws are the hardest to let go of for that reason. It's hard to let go when you know your bad behavior is your own fault. At the end of the day we choose how we react to life, and our egos cause us to act in self-importance. Our personalities, behaviors, and thoughts are all changing. Change within us is constant, and of course it is, certainly you've seen much more of the world than the 13-year-old you had. I've spent the entire book up to this point talking about how modern society is negatively affecting your life. That's all still true, but there is one more culprit to address in your dissatisfaction with life, and it's you.

Yes you. Let's be honest, you aren't innocent here. When I was at my lowest, I was the worst person I ever was. Pointing the finger at everyone else for my problems. Refusing to let go of the smallest injustice against me, if it was even an injustice at all. Ego drives spite. Remember the "fake Pats" - that was my ego. Given I've said the word fifteen times now, let's define it. Ego encompasses our self-perception, particularly regarding our self-importance. Releasing our ego fosters sincerity in our endeavors. When someone is described as having a large ego, it suggests focusing on self-image and external validation rather than genuine passion or joy. Cultivating empathy and compassion requires setting aside ego and adopting The Real Confident You. Religions of the east have known this for centuries. Deepak Chopra has mostly made his career bringing eastern medicine philosophy to the United States. However, I think his greatest contribution has been exposure to Eastern wisdom on the ego like this[94]:

> *"The Ego, however, is not who you really are. The ego is your self-image; it is your social mask; it is the role you are playing. Your social mask thrives on approval. It wants control, and it is sustained by power, because it lives in fear."*

I still struggle with this, remember I am not your guru. We all have an internal drive to impress others. We act inauthentically more than

---

[94] Chopra, Deepak. *The Seven Spiritual Laws of Success*. Amber-Allen Publishing, Incorporated, 2010.

authentically because the fear of the rejection of our true self by others strikes much deeper. We are completely culpable in this. Every time you don't share the realist version of yourself you are telling a lie. To yourself and the people around you. This is where the "real" in "The Real Confident You" comes into play.

Where are friends now right? Don't hold this against me, but I am a work in progress at best. Frankly, you are too. Every person walking this Earth is. Anyone who tells you they aren't is full of shit. And anyone who won't admit that is scared of themselves. Let's work on this together, me and you. I have worked incredibly hard at letting go of my ego and still have a lifetime of work to go. The important part is, we are trying. Acknowledging our wrongs and working to get better. So here we go, let's rip that ego out and stomp it on the ground. As Pharell said, *"The truth will set you free, but first it will piss you off"*[95].

Stop being concerned with other people's opinions

People's opinions about you are reflections of themselves, not of you. However, if you cling to a false sense of identity based on others' views, you'll feel insecure and constantly seek external validation. This dependence on others for validation and ego enhancement is self-destructive. Instead of being swayed by external judgments, turn to yourself. Being self-conscious indicates a lack of self-awareness. If you truly knew yourself, others' opinions wouldn't matter. Self-consciousness reveals that you haven't yet connected with your true self. Only when you stop seeking validation externally and embrace your inner identity can you find peace.

---

[95] Williams, Pharrell. "N.E.R.D & Rihanna – Lemon Lyrics." *Genius*, 1 November 2017, https://genius.com/Nerd-and-rihanna-lemon-lyrics. Accessed 3 April 2024.

Our society seems to only value other people's opinions of us. That's in fact how a society works. It's literally Instagrams business model, make a post and know its worth to the world based on how many "likes" you get. When we let other people's opinions of us decide our worth, we give them the power over who we are. Humans have always had this problem, changing ourselves for the audience around us. Only now the audience is the entire world. That's a lot of validation to seek and can make you feel small very quickly. Not to mention it will never be enough. There will always be a post with more likes, a more glamorous shot, or a better doctored version of a photo. This urge we have to use others to validate the happiness we feel in our own lives must be fought at all costs. <u>Stop being in the passenger seat of your own self-identity.</u> How many things have you not done because other people wouldn't think it's cool? When we are always concerned with the opinions of others, it stops us from living our dreams. To get what you want in life you have to risk your ego and reputation to reach your goals. No one makes the courageous choice for their own life when preoccupied with their reputation.

People will shit on your self-improvement. You just have to get used to that. You will leave people behind if you're really chasing a fulfilling life. Especially in the beginning. No one will see the journey on the horizon like you. But they aren't the ones stuck with the result. It's easy to make judgments when you have no risk. When people give you their suggestions or even orders, there is no risk for them. They don't have to live with your choices—but you do. So don't live with their judgements because they don't have your consequences. Not to mention, most people's opinions are fickle at best. They change like the wind. So why take that judgment into account? If you ask someone what their favorite food, song, movie or tv show is, it will change every 15 minutes. Do you really think their opinion of you isn't subject to change? And even if it is, something that changed that quickly probably isn't that valuable anyway.

Stop treating it as such. Do you know where the term lunatic comes from? It was a derogatory term developed to slander people who thought we could make it to the moon (using the root word luna the name of the Greek goddess of the moon, hence lunar referring to the moon). People trying to do what everyone else isn't have been judged for centuries.

Letting go of others' opinions is not as simple as an exercise. It's a constant check with yourself. Below are a few practices that may help:

Fighting Approval Addiction

1. **Practice Radical Vulnerability:** Going against the norm, voicing dissent, taking risks, or dealing with criticism can be daunting. The most important thing to do is never hide from who you are. Express everything, in full truth, as much as possible. Sure you can't tell your boss you hate your co-workers' guts, but your default expression should be the truth of how you feel. Do so often, make it a point in your life to fully demonstrate your feelings. Additionally, do so with yourself, avoid lying internally to feel comfortable. Your word is your currency, especially with yourself.

2. **Question Yourself:** Know your intentions always. If you were interrupted this morning, could you tell me why you were doing what you were doing? You should be able to. Make your intentions clear, most importantly to yourself. Question your true intentions often. We let our egos take over subconsciously, not consciously. Ice Cube had it right *"You better check yo' self before you wreck yo' self"*[96].

---

[96] Pooh, DJ, and Ice Cube. "Ice Cube – Check Yo Self (Remix) Lyrics." *Genius*, https://genius.com/Ice-cube-check-yo-self-remix-lyrics. Accessed 4 April 2024.

3. **Know your tribe:** Are you surrounded by shallow judgmental people? Get them out. Find the positive ones ASAP.

4. **Don't be so defensive:** Actively listen, practice empathy, and be open to acknowledging mistakes. When we are reflexive with our reactions to defend ourselves we lose autonomy. Making up justifications to defend our actions. When we take accountability, we are much more comfortable with our actions. Also, it leads us to do things differently the next time, for ourselves.

Your Judgment is Just as Bad:

I bet this whole book you've been thinking *"oh I know someone who needs to hear this"*. Congratulations, you are part of the problem. Treat others the way you want to be treated. Remember that little suggestion in Kindergarten? Passing off your own insecurities on someone else through judging them damages you more than it does them. Everyone is doing the best that they can with what they think they have. If it makes someone else happy and harms no one, why the fuck do you care? You have to let go of being a hater, it's making you hate yourself.

Have you been to a comment section on the internet recently? Fucking yikes. The only thing more apparent in our internet driven culture than clout is jealousy and hate. Our judgmental nature is often driven by culture. In Australia and New Zealand their cultures are known for what they call *"Tall Poppy Syndrome"*. It's a phenomenon where accomplished individuals face undo criticism. It arises when their peers perceive them as overly successful or boasting about their achievements[97].

---

[97] Newport Institute. "Tall Poppy Syndrome: When You Get Cut Down for Standing Out." *Newport Institute*, 1 April 2022, https://www.newportinstitute.com/resources/mental-health/tall-poppy-syndrome/. Accessed 4 April 2024.

In a recent survey, 70 percent of respondents indicated that they think Australians generally view ambition negatively[98]. It's such a problem for the Kiwi's and the Roo's an Australian insurance company launched "Tall Poppy," a short film produced by the creators of the Muppets, aimed at addressing Tall Poppy Syndrome[99]. When people are overly critical in Australia and New Zealand it's called "cutting down the tall poppy". Americans didn't typically fall prey to this overly critical view in the past, but times are changing. The internet has made this a worldwide phenomenon, but not just of successes but anything someone may be proud of. If you do something publicly, someone will criticize it. And it spilled over to our personal relationships. We have gotten so deep into our own niches that anyone who is not like us is subject to our scorn. We don't just cut down the tall poppies, we cut down any that aren't like ours. This growing judgmental nature gives us vitriol for anyone who isn't like us.

Often we judge people because we fear what we don't understand. Our brains quickly make judgments that shape our subconscious thoughts, emotions, and behaviors. We all do this and have no control over it. Our subconscious judgments are a natural human reflex. However we do control when our conscious then rationalizes these judgments, often relying on biased, incomplete, or cherry-picked evidence, or even no evidence at all. Uncertainty leads to discomfort and anxiety. This discomfort drives us to seek simple explanations that offer a sense of certainty in an otherwise ambiguous world. We snap judgments as soon as we can. Despite the complexity around us, we tend to perceive ourselves as standing on solid ground of certainty, even as we navigate through a sea of doubt. We would rather have the quick feeling of being

[98] Newport Institute. "Tall Poppy Syndrome: When You Get Cut Down for Standing Out." *Newport Institute*, 1 April 2022, https://www.newportinstitute.com/resources/mental-health/tall-poppy-syndrome/. Accessed 4 April 2024.

[99] Newport Institute. "Tall Poppy Syndrome: When You Get Cut Down for Standing Out." *Newport Institute*, 1 April 2022, https://www.newportinstitute.com/resources/mental-health/tall-poppy-syndrome/. Accessed 4 April 2024.

right than have to understand someone different than us. That is a knee-jerk emotional state, not a thoughtful one. Learning cannot exist without doubt, yet when we refuse to acknowledge doubt, it becomes a harmful force. Our judgements should come after seeking to understand someone, not before. As the ancient Chinese philosopher Laozi said:

"Not-knowing is true knowledge.

Presuming to know is a disease.

First realize that you are sick;

then you can move toward health."

The worst element of judging others is it leads to hating yourself. When we critique others, we condition our minds to detect flaws in them. This habit begins to extend to self-criticism as well. When we set standards on others, we often discover that we fall short of those standards ourselves. Consequently, our inner critic emerges and begins to critique us relentlessly. Judgment of others is mostly an avoidance mechanism for other emotions. From the point of our core emotions we have a choice, either act defensively which manifests in judgment to others and yourself, or empathetically investigate something/someone with an open heart. In every event or situation we are faced with that causes us distress we react in one of two ways.[100].

1. Defend our own ego.

2. Seek to understand before casting judgment.

We choose how to act when distressed. Option one and Option two send us down very different pathways as seen below:

---

[100] Hendel, Hillary Jacobs. "What is The Change Triangle." *Hilary Jacobs Hendel,* https://www.hilaryjacobshendel.com/what-is-the-change-triangle-c18dd. Accessed 5 April 2024.

The Flow of Judgement

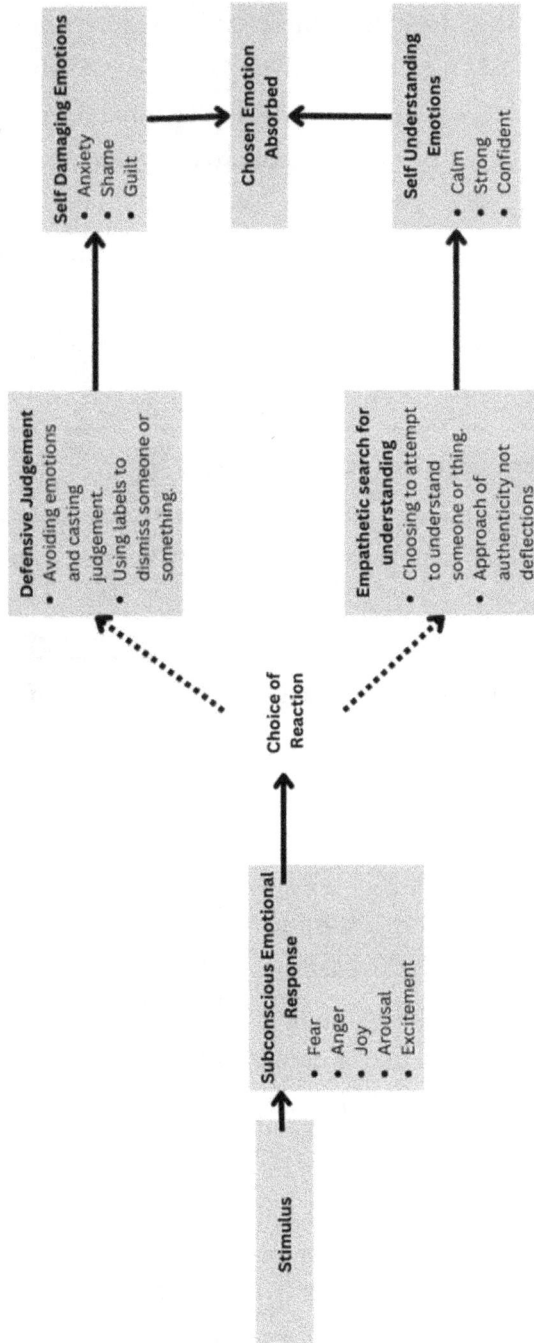

Stimulus

↓

Subconscious Emotional Response
- Fear
- Anger
- Joy
- Arousal
- Excitement

↓

Choice of Reaction

Defensive Judgement
- Avoiding emotions and casting judgement.
- Using labels to dismiss someone or something.

↓

Self Damaging Emotions
- Anxiety
- Shame
- Guilt

→ **Chosen Emotion Absorbed** ←

Self Understanding Emotions
- Calm
- Strong
- Confident

↑

Empathetic search for understanding
- Choosing to attempt to understand someone or thing.
- Approach of authenticity not deflections

When we snap to judge others we miss opportunities to grow while simultaneously hurting ourselves. Let's take the above diagram and go down both scenarios. You can snap to a judgment, and search for an understanding. What we are about to do is kindergarten level basic, trust me I am as aware as you will be in a second. In the scenario below a man named Noah meets someone at a bar. They want to start a conversation, but he notices that they are wearing a T-Shirt promoting a political agenda he does not agree with. He is in town supporting the opposite political agenda.

Stimulus: Conversation with Stranger	
Subconscious Emotional Response: Concern with the character of the stranger	
Option #1 Empathetic search for understanding: Engage in conversation with a stranger.	**Option #2 Defensive Judgment:** Shew the stranger off because you think their ideas are probably idiotic.
Self-Understanding Emotions: You learn about the strangers' viewpoints, and while you may not agree you find they are well intentioned, and you both want a similar end goal.	**Self-Damaging Emotions:** You become angry that someone like that would want to talk to you. How dare they. You think anyone who could think like that is stupid. It upsets you just at the sight of people like that.

Snapping to judgment not only left Noah with a worse perspective, but he was angrier. The ending isn't always perfect when you search for understanding either. Your rational conclusion may be that something is wrong. The person in the scenario above could have been an asshole trying to pick a fight. Still, at least when you seek to understand you can learn that, and know that it's the truth, not a preconceived notion based on judging someone. There are bad people with bad intentions, but more often when we examine something we find that's not the case as often as we think. People have bad days, shit happens, but if you actually try to understand someone their intentions are probably in the right place. A judgment should be formed, not an action of reflex. Sometimes you simply don't have the time to gain an understanding. Honestly, that's most of the time. We can't have a deep philosophical conversation with every person walking the street. You still should try to avoid forming a judgment on someone. Get comfortable with the phrase *"I don't know"*. As Socrates said, *"all I know is that I know nothing"*. Make that your default before jumping to conclusions.

As much as I've lectured here, you shouldn't feel guilty for being judgmental. It's natural, a defense mechanism that's baked in all of us. 100,000 years ago when your ancestors saw someone, they needed to know quickly who they were. If your tribe used red face paint when you saw someone with blue face paint you immediately needed to know if they were your friends or wanted to kill you. That reflex we have serves us no value now. You will come across thousands more people in a year than our ancestors did in their entire lifetime. And trust me 99% of them aren't out to get you. We have to be much better to each other. Here in America especially. Thousands of different cultures intermingling at once, and when we judge everyone not like us it leaves a lonely and self-hate filled existence. Viewing people based on their social stature, money, race or what they like just makes you more unhappy. Embrace the differences in all of us. There is beauty in everyone, start looking for it.

Change your Story, Change your Life

If you were telling the story of your life, what kind of movie would it be? Action, comedy, drama? No matter what the story beats, we chose the narrative of our lives. Let's take two movies, both of them are about a foreigner who comes to America in search of a better life. The protagonists in both movies are criticized for being different, and their bombastic nature gets them in trouble often. In the journey the protagonists lose track of their original reason for coming to America in search of a grand reward. Their lust for the grand reward causes them to lose everything they love in the end. I just described the plotlines of both *Borat* and *Scarface*. *"Pat those movies couldn't be any different, one is about a drug lord and the other about a guy who wears a green thong to the beach and says, 'Very Nice'"*. Of course they are completely different, but their main difference is in how they are told. Borat's search for the love of Pamela Anderson and Scarface's quest to be the cocaine king of Miami are completely different stories. The point is the narrative you make dictates how we perceive a story. What you do to frame a story dictates what our takeaway will be. HOW we are told a story matters much more than the story arch itself.

How do you frame your story? You're writing it right now. When presented with the same facts, our approach can dictate many narratives. You shape that story. It's your leading role. The cast, characters, scenes, they are all your choice. The words are hitting the page, are you writing it? Owning the story lets you tell it how you want. You can interpret the events of your life however you so choose. It's your journey, and you need to take accountability for how it's written. Taking ownership of our story may present challenges, yet it's far less daunting than constantly evading it. Embracing our vulnerabilities involves risks, yet they are nowhere near as perilous as forsaking love, belonging, and joy—the very experiences that expose our truest selves. It's only when we muster the courage to delve into the shadows that we uncover the boundless strength of our inner light.

Accept Help

Our ego often acts as a protective shield, shielding us from perceived threats such as vulnerability and weakness. It convinces us that seeking help is a sign of inadequacy, contradicting its narrative of strength and self-sufficiency. This defense mechanism can lead us to deny the severity of our problems or resist asking for assistance, fearing a loss of control or a dent in our self-image. However, understanding these dynamics can empower us to challenge our ego's barriers and recognize that seeking help is a courageous step towards growth and well-being.

You are not weak for needing help. We all need help, all the time. Nothing can be done alone. Today you drove your car on roads paved by others, to a building you didn't build, to buy products you didn't make. If this book has shown you anything it's you are far from alone. Not taking or asking for help when you need it isn't strong, it's weak. You would rather people think you're ok rather than accept there is something wrong? That's not strength, that's your ego. Accepting help shows how strong you are inside because it means you're aware of your limits and brave enough to ask for support. It takes guts to admit when you need a hand, especially when everyone talks about doing things on their own. When you accept help, you're not just getting advice or assistance; you're also growing as a person and connecting better with others. It's like having a shortcut to solving problems and facing life's twists and turns with more resilience and flexibility, thanks to the people who've got your back.

This doesn't just apply to your mental health. Not taking help at work, school, with your relationships, or in any part of our lives prevents us from improving. There are so many people that care about you and are trying to help, don't shut them out. Even when you think they're wrong, accept that they have good intentions. Advice from someone who cares should always be welcomed, because they are showing great courage in trying to help you.

Help Others

Nothing is more beneficial for us than doing something greater than ourselves. Social media does a fantastic job of making us feel that the world is completely ruthless and we should only look after ourselves. True care and love for each other is at a low. Finding a friend with real intentions is getting harder. That shouldn't stop you from being that friend. The world needs more kindness, so it's on you to be more kind. Don't be the shellfish friend who uses people for your own good. Be a selfless friend.

Pick up the phone when you get a call. Text the person back. Be the person who helps your friend move or will drop everything when they go through a breakup. People don't need more judgment, they need more support. Be the friend you would want. Hug your friends, tell them you love them, and most of all be there to help. Prioritizing others over ourselves is the ultimate display of destroying your ego. The way you talk to others affects your self-image, and the actions you take do too.

Build your Tribe

The thing that I am most proud of in my life are my friends and family. I am the luckiest guy on Earth. My tribe is amazing. But in finding <u>the real confident me</u> I lost a lot of people along the way. It's time for you to leave some people behind too. People who bring you down are not good for you. Negativity is a disease that can spread to you quickly. As much as we try to not let the opinions of others affect us, the people in our lives have a large influence over what we do. You can't fix your friends. Just as you are on your own journey, they are on theirs as well. Writing their own story. If their story is damaging to yours, it's time to move on. You don't need to keep a villain around just because it makes the plot interesting.

Also, you need to seek positive people who are striving for something different. You should always be looking for new people in your life. Expanding our perspective depends on it. Decide what you value in a friendship before you get a new one. Stop looking at people by their social stature, money, beauty etc. Look for friends who will actually enrich your life. Also your friends aren't objects if you have a good one you should value it. I still talk to my best friend from high school every day. He is the funniest son of a bitch I have ever met in my life. Some traditions never graduate. But more so, he has been the most supporting and uplifting person I have ever met. Surround yourself with people like that.

For the Fellas

This section is directed at the male audience. Women, absolutely feel free to stick around for this part as well.

Gentleman. We have a specific problem. We have to seem tough. This may be controversial to say but I am a fan of masculinity. That doesn't mean I think all aspects of us are positive. Far from it. Let's be honest we are getting pretty confusing messaging these days. It seems like half the world thinks a man needs to be a six-foot-tall billionaire womanizer or you provide no value to the world. The other half of the world thinks that anything about being masculine is toxic and any desire you seek is wrong and you are the problem with the world. I get it, it's confusing. Most of all the world would rather see a man die on his white horse than admit there is something wrong.

2/3rds of suicides are men. We don't talk to each other. If any women are still reading, if you are dating a man and you ask him *"what did you and your friend talk about"* and they say, *"nothing really"*, they are not lying. More than likely they spent 4 hours naming obscure running backs from the early 2000s. As men we are conditioned to see any path other than going it alone. The only man I have ever seen go to therapy on T.V. was Tony Soprano, and he was a psychopath killer. In public we are told to hide any weakness, because that's not what being a man is. Well gentleman, it's killing us. It's not popular to talk about but men are struggling more than any time in our conceivable memory. We are graduating from college less, we are lonelier, and our suicide rates are skyrocketing. By all measurable metrics, we are not doing well. These problems we are talking about in the modern world affect us just as much as they do women, but we suffer in silence.

We don't lean on each other for help. Seeming weak to our friends or worse partners feels like the ultimate betrayal. So instead we turn to self-destructive behavior. As men we are much more likely to abuse drugs, alcohol, and all other so-called diseases of despair. Mostly due to how much more backlash we think we will receive at the glimpse of being vulnerable. For men, being seen as weak strikes so much deeper. It's almost like we're less of a person if we show vulnerability. We put all this pressure on ourselves, yet we would never think of it for our friends. We don't look at our friends as weak when tough times hit them, so why do we for ourselves?

It's time for us to change gentlemen. We have to be better for ourselves, and for each other. Perceived weaknesses are not weaknesses. The so-called "tough guy" who doesn't get help with what they're going through isn't tough, it's weak. It's weak to be scared of yourself. Because we don't talk about what we are going through with each other we feel incredibly isolated when we struggle. Think you are alone? Here is a very short list of men who have come out publicly (or we have lost) to talk about their mental health:

Tyson Fury	Kid Cudi	Joesph Goron- Levitt
Mike Tyson	Logic	Robin Williams
Kevin Love	Jon Hamm	Prince
Dwayne "The Rock" Johnson	Brad Pitt	Channing Tatum
	Chris Evans	Owen Wilson
Brandon Marshall	Kanye West	David Goggins
Demar Derozan	Ben Affleck	Chris Bumstead
Michael Phelps	Justin Bieber	Terry Bradshaw
Aaron Rodgers	Jon "Bones" Jones	Oscar De La Hoya
Giannis Antetokounmpo	Lil' Wayne	Dana White
Dak Prescott	Jim Carrey	John Green
Ryan Reynolds	Eminem	Charlamagne Tha God
Pete Wentz	Harrison Ford	
	Chris Kyle	Jay-Z

Call your friends. Check in, say hello. Before you talk about the game, ask how your buddy is doing. Help each other reach your dreams. Put your ego away and start being part of the solution for yourself and friends. And most of all, you are not less of a man when you need their help.

Chapter 11:

Tell Your Story

"Normal is only a setting on the washing machine"
~ **Brittany Crammond**

This entire book has been about helping your own journey to get better. In reality, you have overcome so much more than the world will ever know before opening this book. I hope you think that what you've read so far is money well spent, but nothing is as powerful as the force you already are. There is no self-help book as powerful as your own story. I think this genre as a whole has been flawed for quite some time. One person telling you the way the world works like they have all the answers to fix your problems. Some titles like *10 steps to change your life* with some generic self-improvement tips. The problem is one person's experience is not as powerful as the masses. Every single one of us has overcome a challenge that no one else has, yet we don't share it.

We can't fix all of the problems in the world by ourselves. But we can do our best to improve what's around us. You have already been The Real Confident You more times than you can count. You have so much to be proud of. The things you have overcome up to this point are nothing to hide from. The modern world makes it seem like everyone is shiny and happy while we struggle alone. That's bullshit. It's not real. It's time for all of us to stop struggling alone behind a screen. I'm fucking done filtering my true self through the filter of the world, aren't you? You ESPECIALLY have an unequivocal duty to approach the world with kindness. We change the world with the people around us. Kindness, love, empathy, they are all contagious. They just need someone to spread them. And that starts with you.

Years after I laid on that cold bathroom floor with the realization that life was worth living and changed my life there was one thing missing. I was happy, had great friendships, was fulfilled in my career and was able to be myself through all of it. The puzzle still was missing one piece, sharing the truth. Being The Real Confident You starts with you but should benefit the world around you. The years spent improving myself were just that about myself. While I fully believe being your best self is to the benefit of everyone around you, your best self doesn't hide from the truth. We all have a box of secrets we keep in our closet. We are too embarrassed to admit we have been through something hard for fear of being judged. That fear inside of us has created a mass disease of inauthenticity. We have all become brands that anything seeming to tarnish would make us less valuable. It lets superficiality rise to the top of our feeds, online and in life.

The final step in becoming The Real Confident You is telling your story. Your story doesn't need to be as drastic as mine or maybe it's even more drastic. But the people around us need to know they are not alone from people they actually know and love. You are a badass who has overcome more than anyone around you even has a glimpse of understanding. And if you have not overcome it, you are going through something right now. Your world needs to hear that. We all need more of that. Authenticity. The feeling of not being alone needs to be more than a statistic, or a celebrity advocating on T.V.. It needs to be us, sharing with each other what we are going through and lifting each other up.

What is my story?

You have struggled with something in your life. It's the universal truth for all of us. No one's life is a story without some sort of hardship. Don't limit yourself to mental health, maybe it's financial, physical, or a life event that brought you significant strain. The point being we often don't let people really know what we are going through in our hardest moments. What we do (or are currently doing) to overcome them is a vessel to change our little corner of the world. We are all inspirations. We limit inspirations to great athletes or insane achievers, but inspirational stories are all around us. When we don't share them, we starve our people of their chances to be inspired. Hiding our struggles can be detrimental to our well-being in several ways. It prevents us from receiving the support and understanding what we may need from others. When we conceal our challenges, we miss out on opportunities for empathy, advice, and encouragement that can help us navigate difficult times. Additionally, hiding our struggles can lead to feelings of isolation and loneliness, as we may believe that we are the only ones facing such difficulties. This isolation can worsen our mental health and hinder our ability to cope effectively. Moreover, concealing our struggles can create a facade of perfection, leading to added pressure to maintain this image and increasing stress levels. Ultimately, being open about our struggles fosters authenticity, strengthens connections with others, and promotes a healthier approach to facing life's challenges. That approach could be called The Real Confident You.

Social media can often contribute to the tendency to hide or distort our stories. The pressure to present an idealized version of ourselves online, curated with only the highlights and successes. We fear judgment, rejection, or negative comparisons if we reveal our vulnerabilities or struggles. This pressure to maintain a perfect image can lead to feelings of inadequacy and a sense of isolation, as we believe that others' lives are flawless compared to our own. We prioritize superficiality and instant gratification, encouraging us to showcase only the positive aspects of our lives. This creates a disconnect between our online personas and our authentic selves, making it challenging to share our true stories openly.

Moreover, the fear of backlash or criticism on social media platforms can also contribute to hiding our stories. The fear of being misunderstood can deter us from being vulnerable and sharing our struggles authentically. And while this problem is one of social media, our warped perception makes it impossible for that authenticity to come out in real life either.

Your story can be anything that you have struggled with. We all face challenges in life that shape who we are. Your story of struggle, perseverance, and eventual triumph is not just yours; it's a beacon of hope and inspiration for others. By sharing your experiences, you not only validate your journey but also offer a lifeline to those who may be navigating similar paths. Your courage to be vulnerable can ignite a spark of resilience in someone else's heart. Choosing which story to share is a deeply personal decision. Consider selecting a story that has shaped you significantly, one that highlights your growth, resilience, and the lessons you've learned along the way. Reflect on how this story can inspire others, offering insights, empathy, or a sense of solidarity. Remember that sharing your story is not about showcasing perfection but about sharing authenticity and connecting with others on a human level. Trust your instincts and choose a narrative that feels genuine and meaningful to you.

How do I tell my story?

Sharing a part of you know one has ever heard before is scary. Doing so publicly is even scarier. That is not what I am going to ask you to do. I am asking you to develop a story for your chosen audience.

To develop a story about your personal struggle, start by reflecting on the key moments, emotions, and challenges you faced during that time. Begin with an introduction that sets the stage for your struggle, providing context and background information. Then, delve into the details of your journey, highlighting the obstacles you encountered, the emotions you experienced, and the strategies you used to cope and overcome. Be honest, vulnerable, and authentic in sharing your story to create a deeper connection with your audience. Finally, conclude your story by reflecting on the lessons learned, the growth achieved, and the impact of the experience on your life.

Developing a story about your personal struggle is quite therapeutic. It helps you make sense of what you've been through, gain clarity and understanding, and recognize your strengths and resilience. It provides a safe outlet for expressing emotions, releasing pent-up feelings, and letting go of negative thoughts or beliefs associated with the struggle. When you share your story, it also connects you with others who may have similar experiences, fostering empathy, support, and a sense of belonging. Plus, it gives you a safe space to express your emotions, release any pent-up feelings, and ultimately promote healing and closure.

To develop a story about your personal struggle, start by reflecting on the key moments, emotions, and challenges you faced during that time. Begin with an introduction that sets the stage for your struggle, providing context and background information. Then, delve into the details of your journey, highlighting the obstacles you encountered, the emotions you experienced, and the strategies you used to cope and overcome. Be honest, vulnerable, and authentic in sharing your story to create a deeper connection with your audience. Finally, conclude your story by reflecting on the lessons learned, the growth achieved, and the impact of the experience on your life.

Sharing your story doesn't have to be some big public display like mine. While that may have the chance of helping more people, I completely understand your hesitation. The point of telling your story isn't a grand moment. It's getting something off your chest, and inspiring others along the way. Yes, a social media post, article, or anything public about what you have been through is awesome. But doing something on a smaller scale is just as valid. It can look like:

- Confiding in friends or family
- Having a share session with your partner
- Putting out an anonymous piece of content

The point is to finally become <u>The Real Confident You</u> here has to be a moment to help others. Be the opposite of the social media world. Share your truest self. Feel no shame in your struggle or failures, wear it like a badge of honor. Your people need "<u>The Real Confident You</u>", will you help them?

A Community of Hope

Before you donate this book I just want to let you know how extremely thankful I am that you took the time to read this. Being this is my first book, you may be one of seven people who buys it, so thank you.

I am always here. My contact info is in the back of this book. Reach out whenever, I will always be happy to talk (even if you want to tell me I am full of shit). Oh, and if you happen to tell your story publicly, tag me, I would love to share it.

Contact the Author: Pat Broe

LinkedIn: www.linkedin.com/in/patrick-broe

Instagram: @patbroe

Email: therealconfidentyou@gmail.com

www.ingramcontent.com/pod-product-compliance
Lightning Source LLC
LaVergne TN
LVHW041316080426
835513LV00008B/486

9 781950 336852